Influencers, Activists,
and Women's Rights

CARMEN DE BURGOS SEGUÍ
("COLOMBINE")

Influencers, Activists, and Women's Rights

A Translation of
DIVORCE IN SPAIN

EDITED BY
Rebecca M. Bender

TRANSLATED BY
Slava Faybysh

The Modern Language Association of America
New York   2024

© 2024 by The Modern Language Association of America
85 Broad Street, New York, New York 10004
www.mla.org

To order MLA publications, visit www.mla.org/books. For wholesale and
international orders, see www.mla.org/bookstore-orders.

The MLA office is located on the island known as Mannahatta (Manhattan)
in Lenapehoking, the homeland of the Lenape people. The MLA pays
respect to the original stewards of this land and to the diverse and vibrant
Native communities that continue to thrive in New York City.

Cover illustration: María Blanchard, *Femme à la guitare*, 1917, Museo
Nacional Centro de Arte Reina Sofía.

Texts and Translations 45

ISSN 1079-2538

Library of Congress Cataloging-in-Publication Data

Names: Burgos, Carmen de, 1867–1932, author. | Bender, Rebecca M.,
    editor. | Faybysh, Slava, translator.
Title: Influencers, activists, and women's rights : a translation of Divorce
    in Spain / Carmen de Burgos Seguí ("Colombine") ; edited by
    Rebecca M. Bender ; translated by Slava Faybysh.
Other titles: Divorcio en España. English
Description: New York : The Modern Language Association of America,
    2024. | Series: Texts and translations, 1079-2538 ; 45 | Includes
    bibliographical references.
Identifiers: LCCN 2024013115 (print) | LCCN 2024013116 (ebook) |
    ISBN 9781603296694 (paperback) | ISBN 9781603296700 (EPUB)
Subjects: LCSH: Divorce—Spain.
Classification: LCC HQ916 .B813 2024 (print) | LCC HQ916 (ebook) |
    DDC 306.890946—dc23/eng/20240606
LC record available at https://lccn.loc.gov/2024013115
LC ebook record available at https://lccn.loc.gov/2024013116

Contents

INTRODUCTION: FROM SCANDAL TO INFLUENCER TO ACTIVIST: CARMEN DE BURGOS, "COLOMBINE"

Carmen de Burgos Seguí,[1] popularly known by her pen name, "Colombine," is one of the key figures to emerge in Spanish feminist thought and activism at the beginning of the twentieth century. Along with her massive literary and journalistic output, throughout her life she took on diverse professional roles and projects based on almost any topic that interested her. She was a teacher, translator, editor, novelist, short story writer, and journalist; she wrote beauty manuals, cookbooks, feminist treatises, travelogues, and editorials on human rights issues such as prison reform, maternal and infant mortality rates, and divorce. She was also one of the most cosmopolitan Spanish women of her time, boasting an impressive résumé of international travel that included Argentina, Mexico, Peru, Chile, Brazil, Cuba, Bolivia, Panama, Portugal, Morocco, England, France, Switzerland, Italy, Norway, Denmark, and Germany (Mangini 62). Unfortunately, Burgos's extensive literary output, produced largely between 1900 and 1932, was overlooked for nearly half a century because of the censorship of Francisco Franco's fascist dictatorship, which ruled from 1939 to 1975. In fact, Burgos was included among the first ten novelists and journalists prohibited by Franco's regime, joining the likes of Émile Zola, Voltaire, Jean-Jacques Rousseau, and Upton Sinclair (Núñez Rey, *Carmen de Burgos, Colombine en la Edad de Plata* 624–25). As Concepción Núñez Rey eloquently notes, the memory of Burgos and the impact she had on Spanish culture remained hidden in the depths of library archives, as though a volcano had suddenly buried a flourishing city under its ashes (10). The first study on her literary production and cultural impact did not occur until 1976 (Starcevic), and it is only today, more than eighty years after the censorship of her work by the Franco regime, that scholars are reexamining her writing (see Louis and Sharp), republishing her novels with modern Spanish presses, and translating her words into English.

Divorce in Spain is the result of one of Burgos's first initiatives as a columnist for *Diario Universal* (*Universal Daily*), one of Madrid's most prestigious, liberal-leaning newspapers in the early twentieth century. This book-length publication, translated into English for the first time here, is the result of a survey that Burgos published in late 1903, calling for editorials reflecting her readers' opinions on divorce. After receiving hundreds of responses, she compiled those of high-profile individuals and published them together as *Divorce in Spain* in 1904. This early publication is unique in Burgos's literary oeuvre, as she did not write the full text herself but rather compiled the writings of others, edited them into a cohesive volume, and added her own introduction and commentary. *Divorce in Spain* reflects Spanish public opinion on the definition and purpose of divorce in Spain's legal codes, but it also contains a few contributions from Burgos herself, in which she argues for divorce reform. For example, her clever essay "El divorcio de las monjas" ("The Divorce of Nuns") cheekily proposes that if Catholic nuns could renounce their vows and divorce the most perfect of all husbands (Jesus Christ), then Spanish women should certainly be permitted to divorce their mortal, imperfect spouses. As a result of her brave initiative, *Divorce in Spain* prompted public debate on a contentious topic related to the early women's movement.

This brief introduction contextualizes Burgos's engagement with polemical women's issues in early-twentieth-century Spain and with first-wave feminist thought. It uses key moments and roles from Burgos's professional and personal biography as links to her lifelong advocacy for women's education and increased legal rights. Importantly, this introduction clarifies the meaning of divorce in late-nineteenth-century Spanish legal codes, as the Spanish word *divorcio* had slightly different meanings and connotations at that time than its English equivalent now has.

Burgos and Early Spanish Feminism

While today she is most closely associated with the bustling intellectual culture of Spain's rapidly modernizing capital city, Madrid, in the early 1900s, Burgos was born in 1867 in Rodalquilar, a rural Andalusian *pueblo* ("village") near the southern Spanish city of Almería. Against the advice of her family, she married a man fifteen years her senior when she was a mere sixteen years of age. The marriage was not a happy one: her husband had difficulty keeping a job, was irresponsible with money, and was abusive and unfaithful to his wife (Ballarín Domingo 17). Out of necessity, Burgos began to supplement her family's income by working for her father-in-law's newspaper, which exposed her to the intricacies of the world of journalism and publishing for the first time. By the age of thirty, she had given birth to four children, but only one daughter survived infancy. Anja Louis suggests that the death of Burgos's eight-month-old son in 1894 marked a turning point in the future writer's provincial Almerían lifestyle (4). Burgos promptly enrolled in university courses in Granada and obtained teaching credentials by 1895, thanks to Spain's late-nineteenth-century educational reforms. As she began to earn her own income as a teacher near Rodalquilar, she saved enough to finally leave her husband and take a teaching job in Guadalajara, outside Madrid. Her decision to abandon her husband was not without controversy, especially in a conservative, rural Spanish town whose residents held intensely Catholic values. Pilar Ballarín Domingo suggests that rampant gossip and slander about the unhappy marriage and the wife's increasing independence may have accelerated Burgos's departure for Madrid (18). Shirley Mangini believes that such a scandal could scarcely have been greater in a traditional village: a married woman had abandoned her husband to move to the capital city, taking their child with her (60).[2]

For Burgos, and for ambitious, educated women like her, Madrid represented a new beginning, one that offered great freedom and promise for her ability to succeed as a writer. At the turn of the early twentieth century, European cities were expanding and transforming into modern, commercial societies. This afforded women like Burgos the opportunity for paid employment in the public sphere, which came with a liberating sense of independence and anonymity that was impossible in small towns. When she relocated to Madrid in August 1901, Burgos established contact with the intellectual world and developed professional relationships with some of Madrid's top journals and newspapers, including *Diario Universal*, *ABC*, and *Heraldo de Madrid* (*Madrid Herald*). While she arrived in the city with no certain prospects for steady employment, she was lucky enough to be able to count on family contacts to obtain work as a teacher with Madrid's School for Arts and Industry (Mangini 60). In 1903 she began publishing a regular column, "Lecturas para mujeres" ("Readings for Women"), in the prestigious *Diario Universal*. It was the director of this newspaper who gave her the pseudonym Colombine, a playful pen name that she would retain throughout her career, not to hide her identity, but rather to appeal to working-class readers (Kirkpatrick 172). "Colombine" alludes to an intelligent, cheeky maid that was a popular character in French and Italian theater, but the name was also a sign of femininity, female cunning and frivolity, and cosmopolitan modernism (172–73). Burgos's willingness to adopt this epithet indicates, according to Susan Kirkpatrick, that she valued the class identity of the witty servant character as a means of linking her own increasingly public persona to the liberal, democratic spirit that was emerging among the urban middle and working classes (173). From these early days in Madrid, Burgos worked to establish a relationship with her readers by identifying with them, and she positioned herself among their ranks by including her own identity and lived experiences in her writing (Ugarte 61). Through her columns in *Diario Universal*, she was able to educate the public about legal and social issues, especially those concerning women.

In a sense, we might say that Burgos took to Madrid to participate in its far-reaching print culture the way that twenty-first-century influencers take to Los Angeles or New York to deploy the power of their identities and brands on popular platforms like *Instagram*, *YouTube*, or *TikTok*. Her control over "Readings for Women" gave her access to a large audience of predominantly female readers. Her role as editor afforded her a degree of authority, while her knowledge, personal experiences, professional position, and carefully cultivated relationship with her audience granted her a uniquely modern influence over her readers' opinions. As a writer and journalist, she frequented the most exclusive, male-dominated intellectual and avant-garde circles of her time, even establishing her own popular *tertulia* ("social gathering") in Madrid in 1906, *Los miércoles de Colombine* ("Colombine's Wednesdays"). Like today's influencers, Burgos aimed to engage her audience by publishing hot-button content that would raise awareness and prompt discussions on evolving social or cultural issues. This was the case with divorce, and in late 1903 Burgos began surveying her regular readers, or followers, and suggested that a "club de matrimonios mal avenidos" ("Club of Unhappily Married Couples") be formed in Madrid to study the Spanish divorce laws and present an argument for their reform in parliament. She immediately received letters supporting this endeavor, and the swift replies prompted her to launch a poll requesting the opinions of her readership and of Spain's most eminent literary and political personalities. Among the most prominent intellectuals who responded were the novelist, poet, and philosopher Miguel de Unamuno, the novelist Pío Baroja, and the early feminist novelist and essayist Emilia Pardo Bazán. As high-profile responses to her query continued to arrive over the following months, Burgos selected contributions to publish weekly in *Diario Universal* then compiled them into a cohesive volume published as *Divorce in Spain* in 1904. This ongoing project on divorce was enormously popular and, not surprisingly, controversial. In publicizing and promoting debate on divorce, Burgos "manifested a lack of respect for and adherence to the Catholic Church, a cornerstone of middle-class Spanish women's existence and the public expression of their moral character" (Bermúdez and Johnson 178).[3] Consequently, she earned a new nickname, "La divorciadora" ("the Divorcer"), which was pejoratively used to challenge her authority and smear her reputation. Today we might say that this hashtag-worthy moniker was deployed in a failed attempt to "cancel" her or to discredit her arguments and stifle her ambitions.

Colombine the Divorcer, however, refused to remain silent on the issue. In fact, her advocacy for reforming Spanish laws on spousal separation and the status of married women reappeared in her writing and activism throughout her career, likely fueled by her own negative experiences as a young wife and mother in an unhappy, abusive marriage. In addition to *Divorce in Spain*, her newspaper columns, and subsequent essays, Burgos also wrote fiction that dealt with unhappy marriages, discrimination against married women in the legal codes, and the need for divorce reform. In 1921, for example, she published "El artículo 438" ("Article 438"), a novelette that critiques the abusive Spanish legal system, whose article 438—dating to the 1870 penal codes—inscribed adultery as a crime and permitted a husband to kill his wife if he discovered her in the act; there was no such law for a husband's transgressions. The adulterous protagonist in this novelette engages in an extramarital affair that provides fleeting happiness, but rather than chastise her, the narrative highlights her suffering and victimization within both her marriage and the legal system.[4] In 1923 Burgos published a full-length novel, *La malcasada* (*The Unhappily Married Woman*), featuring a protagonist who is a victim of both an abusive husband and the Spanish legal system, dual powers that force her to remain trapped in her marriage. Several scholars have pointed to clear autobiographical elements within this novel, and Louis describes it as reading "like a case study out of a law textbook" (44). These two fictional narratives exposed the double standards of the Spanish civil and penal codes, raised awareness of inequitable patriarchal practices, and helped set the stage for legal reform. According to Silvia Bermúdez and Roberta Johnson, "no other Spanish feminist thinker in Burgos's own generation . . . argues for their feminist program from a strictly legal point of view" (228). Spanish legal discourse at the time was "predominantly a male enterprise," and, while Burgos had no legal training, she took the perspective of an "informed layperson" and positioned herself as an intermediary between the legal profession and the public (Louis 34). As a writer, lecturer, activist, and feminist, Burgos championed reform of the most oppressive and antiquated aspects of the civil and penal codes, most notably the arbitrary, gendered nature of legal discourse.[5]

The focus on the position of women within the legal system is key to understanding Burgos's goals in *Divorce in Spain*. Given her own unhappy marriage and the reformist sentiment that prompted her survey, it may be surprising to learn that Burgos was not opposed to the institution of marriage. While some anarchists or radical feminists in other nations may have viewed marriage as rooted in inequality and a power imbalance, Burgos pointed instead to the measurable loss of human rights experienced by women within the legal frameworks of the institution; she even believed that feminism was in favor of marriage (Louis 27). In early-twentieth-century Spain, women had limited choices in terms of their future. If they remained unmarried, they might become social outcasts, but if they married, which was expected and encouraged, their legal subjectivity would be akin to that of minors, as their husbands controlled their finances, legal rights, and even the custody of their children (65–66). Burgos insisted that women resisted marriage not because they were disinterested in or did not love men but rather because they knew that their civil rights would be severely restricted as soon as they said "I do" (41). As she would later point out in her lengthy feminist treatise, *La mujer moderna y sus derechos* (*On Modern Women and Their Rights*), the problem resided in the discrepancy between the civil codes, which limited the rights of a married woman and required her to obey her husband, and the Constitution, which affirmed the equality of all Spaniards. She demonstrates that under the legal codes, when adult women married, their legal status was redefined to be similar to that of minors and, in some cases, people who were blind, deaf, or mentally ill (Burgos 165).

Yet Burgos was not exactly a radical feminist crusader of the kind we may imagine today. In fact, some of her early positions may appear conservative when compared to our twenty-first-century understanding of feminism in the Anglosphere and even to first-wave feminist initiatives in other western European nations. Within the parameters of first-wave feminism—meaning early feminist activity between the 1850s and the 1960s, when middle-class women in North America and western Europe began to organize in order to exert influence on public life and achieve personal autonomy (LeGates 197)—Spanish feminist thought has been classified as slower to progress.[6] This is because Spain was a unique microcosm, isolated both geographically and culturally from the radical changes occurring in other Western nations. This moderate seclusion contributed to a more conservative culture with regards to the women's movement—or the "problema feminista" ("feminist problem"; Mangini 93; my trans.), as it was known in Spain. The Pyrenees Mountains separate the Iberian Peninsula from the rest of Europe, meaning Spain (and Portugal) occupy peripheral spaces. Culturally, the enormous influence of Catholicism over Spanish society, and especially over Spanish women, meant that Catholic institutions and dogma presented obstacles to feminist reforms in Spain (Scanlon 5–7; Ugarte 62). In addition, Mary Nash classifies first-wave Spanish feminism as predominantly social in orientation, and first-wave Spanish feminists privileged social issues like access to education, divorce, and equal pay above political rights like suffrage and government involvement (20). In fact, many Spanish women—including Burgos very early in her career—were opposed to women's suffrage, fearing that the poor education and religiosity of women would lead them to simply duplicate the votes of patriarchal powers such as their husbands, fathers, or priests (Bender 133). Similarly, not all women supported divorce reform, because they feared that men would be the benefactors of a modernized law, gaining the right to abandon a woman, leave her without income or protection, and even take her children, as Spanish law already gave preference to the father in the custody of children.

Divorce, Separation, and the Spanish Legal Codes

In reading *Divorce in Spain*, we must recognize that the word *divorcio*—which did indeed appear in Spain's Civil Code of 1889—did not mean "divorce" in the same way that we use the word today. Louis explains that *divorcio* in the civil code referred only to the legal separation of spouses and did not allow for the full dissolution of a marriage (22). The legal separation freed women from "conjugal demands" on their bodies, disentangled finances so that women could retain monies they may have brought into the marriage, and established legal custody for any children between the marriage partners (Bieder 30). The grounds for legal separation, however, were limited, focusing on the adultery of the wife (or the husband, if it caused a public scandal), serious injuries or violence inflicted on one partner by another, attempts by the husband to prostitute his wife or corrupt his children, and the condemnation of a partner to a life sentence (Sponsler 1616–17). Given that a legal separation did not actually dissolve the marriage, neither party could remarry while their separated spouse was still alive (Bermúdez and Johnson 177). Moreover, the legal codes left no room for spousal separation in cases where the woman was unhappy, no longer loved her husband, or desired simply to change her lifestyle of her own volition. And if children were born of the marriage, the father had priority in terms of custody since women had inferior status in the era's civil codes, akin to that of minors (Bieder 30). Given the restrictive definition of and justifications for *divorcio* ("separation") in the legal codes, Burgos's survey was meant to open debate on divorce with the goal of reforming the laws so that unhappy or abusive marriages could be entirely dissolved. In reading the English translation of *Divorce in Spain*, we must keep in mind that the writers and intellectuals who responded to Burgos's opinion poll were all using the term *divorce* to refer to the modernization of an existing premise of marriage separation. Opinions in favor of divorce, then, centered on reforming the legal definition to include the full dissolution of a marriage, the right of both parties to remarry, and the expansion of the reasons that either partner in a marriage might seek a divorce.

In concluding *Divorce in Spain*, Burgos tallies the nearly 1,800 responses: 1,462 in favor of reforming the laws and 320 against. She summarizes the results, listing concise reasons for the need to reform divorce in the Spanish legal system. First, she connects a potential modernized definition of divorce, as the full dissolution of a marriage, to progress by noting its legality in most developed countries. Second, she argues that dissolving marriages under a new divorce law would be advantageous to society and to morals, particularly as private morality should remain independent of public legislation. Finally, she quantifies the data to prove that the number of responses in favor of reform far outnumber those against, a clear indication that Spanish opinion was favorable to more progressive divorce laws. The most liberal comments focused on modernizing or civilizing Spain, while the most conservative centered on the potential threat that divorce reform could pose to the family unit and children. Some responses were noncommittal but nevertheless engaged with issues of love, morality, and social reform. One of the most repeated themes was the concern for the family as the basis of a healthy Spanish society. Those who advocated for divorce reform were viewed suspiciously by their opponents, as enemies of traditional family values, while those who opposed more liberal divorce rights feared that dissolved marriages and subsequent remarriages would lead to the breakdown of society or moral anarchy (Louis 27–28). As such, early divorce debates in Spain revolved around whose interests should be prioritized: the individual's desires or society's interest in protecting the traditional family unit, or nuclear family in today's terminology (29).

All in all, *Divorce in Spain* prompted lively public debate and feminist engagement that would last for thirty years before the eventual progressive reform of the civil codes that women like Burgos so desired. Modern divorce—the full dissolution of a marriage at the request of one or both parties, along with the right to remarry—was first legalized in Spain under the progressive Second Republic in 1931, in the form of article 43 of the Constitution, which states, "Marriage is based on equal rights for both sexes and can be dissolved by mutual wish or petition of either one of the parties" (Bermúdez and Johnson 218). The Divorce Act of 1932 was introduced only a few months later, following the guidelines established in the Constitution to formalize the legality of divorce. Carmen de Burgos, or Colombine the Divorcer, lived just long enough to witness this milestone in the struggle for women's legal rights—the passage of the revised divorce laws for which she and other feminist writers, intellectuals, and activists had so adamantly advocated. She died in 1932, only a few months after the ratification of the Divorce Act under the Spanish Republic, and a popular legend arose of her collapse at a roundtable discussion where she uttered her final words: "¡Viva la República!" ("Long live the Republic!";

Ballarín Domingo 33; my trans.). Unfortunately, the new republican government's achievements would be short-lived, and divorce became illegal again in April 1938, when members of the Spanish Nationalist Party repealed the legislation—one of the first pieces to be eliminated—before the end of the Spanish Civil War, in 1939 (Louis 66). The ensuing dictatorship of Francisco Franco reinforced the same nineteenth-century civil codes that had become antiquated in the early twentieth century, thus reestablishing the supremacy of a husband over his wife in marriage and banning divorce (as the dissolution of a marriage) from the Spanish legal system for another forty years. It was not until 1981 that men and women were declared equal in marriage and a new divorce law was passed to allow for the full dissolution of marriages.[7]

Notes

1. Full Spanish names are typically composed of two surnames, optionally separated by the conjunction *y* ("and"). The first surname is almost always the father's first surname, and the second one, which is often dropped, is the mother's first surname. For instance, "Carmen de Burgos Seguí" is the writer's full legal name, but Burgos typically drops "Seguí."

2. Her less honorable status as a "separated wife" would improve in 1905 upon the death of her estranged husband, which afforded her a more respectable civil status as a widow (Louis 5).

3. Burgos even admitted in a 1916 interview that *Divorce in Spain* had been her most controversial and divisive work to date, given that it attacked sanctimoniousness, prudishness, and religious bigotry (Núñez Rey, *Carmen de Burgos, Colombine, periodista* 241).

4. See Doyle for a summary of article 438 and for an analysis of Burgos's novelette and its use of this article as a basis to explore women's rights and sexual desire. Article 438 was only amended in 1928 and finally repealed in 1932.

5. See Louis for an analysis of the Spanish legal codes and public discourse surrounding them. Louis highlights Burgos's role in reforming the most misogynous penal and civil codes, like article 438, through critiques carefully crafted in the writer's essays and melodramatic fiction.

6. Even though feminism was a frequent topic in Spanish journals, newspapers, and public conferences during the early 1900s, it was not until the end of the 1920s that Spanish women began to organize into groups proposing coherent programs of reform (Scanlon 4–5). For Scanlon, by the time feminism "arrived" in Spain, it appeared domesticated in comparison with the radical struggles and demonstrations of suffragettes in other countries (196).

7. See Sponsler for details regarding divorce and married women's status in the Spanish legal codes from the early twentieth century through the 1981 Divorce Law.

Works Cited

Ballarín Domingo, Pilar. Introduction. Burgos, pp. 13–54.

Bender, Rebecca M. "Theorizing a Hybrid Feminism: Motherhood in Margarita Nelken's *En torno a nosotras.*" *Bulletin of Hispanic Studies*, vol. 93, no. 2, 2016, pp. 131–48.

Bermúdez, Silvia, and Roberta Johnson, editors. *A New History of Iberian Feminisms.* U of Toronto P, 2018.

Bieder, Maryellen. "The Carmen de Burgos Enigma: Marriage, Separation, and Public Activism." Louis and Sharp, pp. 27–42.

Burgos, Carmen de. *La mujer moderna y sus derechos.* Edited by Pilar Ballarín Domingo, Biblioteca Nueva, 2007.

Doyle, Kathleen. "Body of Evidence: The Legislation of Female Desire in 'El artículo 438' by Carmen de Burgos." *Letras Femeninas*, vol. 30, no. 1, 2004, pp. 155–64. *JSTOR*, www.jstor.org/stable/23021429.

Kirkpatrick, Susan. *Mujer, modernismo y vanguardia en España, 1898–1931.* Translated by Jacqueline Cruz, Cátedra, 2003.

LeGates, Marlene. *In Their Time: A History of Feminism in Western Society.* Routledge, 2001.

Louis, Anja. *Women and the Law: Carmen de Burgos, an Early Feminist.* Tamesis, 2005.

Louis, Anja, and Michelle M. Sharp, editors. *Multiple Modernities: Carmen de Burgos, Author and Activist.* Routledge, 2017.

Mangini, Shirley. *Las modernas de Madrid: Las grandes intelectuales españolas de la vanguardia.* Ediciones Península, 2001.

Nash, Mary. "Género, cambio social y la problemática del aborto." *Historia Social*, vol. 2, 1988, pp. 19–35.

Núñez Rey, Concepción. *Carmen de Burgos, Colombine en la Edad de Plata de la literatura española.* Fundación José Manuel Lara, 2005.

———. *Carmen de Burgos, Colombine, periodista universal.* Junta de Andalucía, Consejería Cultural, 2018. 2 vols.

Scanlon, Geraldine M. *La polémica feminista en la España contemporánea, 1898–1974.* Translated by Rafael Mazarrasa, Akal, 1986.

Sponsler, Lucy A. "The Status of Married Women under the Legal System of Spain." *Louisiana Law Review,* vol. 42, no. 5, 1982, pp. 1599–628, digitalcommons.law.lsu.edu/cgi/viewcontent.cgi?article=4684&context=lalrev.

Starcevic, Elizabeth. *Carmen de Burgos, defensora de la mujer.* Librería-Editorial Cajal, 1976.

Ugarte, Michael. "Carmen de Burgos ('Colombine'): Feminist *avant la Lettre.*" *Spanish Women Writers and the Essay: Gender, Politics and the Self,* edited by Kathleen Mary Glenn and Mercedes Mazquiarán de Rodríguez, U of Missouri P, 1998, pp. 55–74.

Selected Works by Carmen de Burgos

Novels

Los inadaptados (*The Misfits*, 1909)
La rampa (*The Ramp*, 1917)
El último contrabandista (*The Last Smuggler*, 1918)
La malcasada (*The Unhappily Married Woman*, 1923)
Quiero vivir mi vida (*I Want to Live My Life*, 1931)

Novelettes

"El veneno del arte" ("The Poison of Art," 1910)
"Villa María" (1916)
"Los míseros" ("Stingy People," 1916)
"El perseguidor" ("The Stalker," 1917)
"¡Todos menos ese!" ("Anybody but Him!," 1918)
"Luna de miel" ("The Honeymoon," 1921)
"El artículo 438" ("Article 438," 1921)
"Los huesos del abuelo" ("Grandfather's Bones," 1922)
"La princesa rusa" ("The Russian Princess," 1923)[1]
"El silencio del hijo" ("A Son's Silence," 1925)
"Puñal de claveles" ("A Dagger of Carnations," 1931)

---

1. Translated by Slava Faybysh, in *Virginia's Sisters*, edited by Gabi Reigh, 2023.

Essays, Manuals, Travelogues, and Biographies

Ensayos literarios (*Literary Essays*, 1900)

Por Europa (*Around Europe*, 1906)

En la guerra (*In the War*, 1909)

Las artes de la mujer (*A Woman's Skills*, 1911)

Impresiones de Argentina (*Impressions of Argentina*, 1914)

Mis viajes por Europa (*My Travels through Europe*, 1917)

¿Quiere usted comer bien? Manual práctico de cocina (*Do You Want to Eat Well? A Practical Cooking Manual*, 1917)

La cocina moderna (*Modern Cooking*, ca. 1918)

Fígaro (1919)

El arte de ser mujer (*The Art of Being a Woman*, ca. 1920)

La mujer moderna y sus derechos (*On Modern Women and Their Rights*, 1927)[2]

---

2. Translated by Gabriela Pozzi and Keith Watts, 2018.

NOTE ON THE TRANSLATION

A meme has been circulating recently about how to properly translate office emails. It explains that the phrase "per my last email" actually means "Can't you read? I already told you this." "Not sure if my last email was received" means "Just how long do you think you can ignore me?" "To put it more simply" means "Are you seriously that stupid?" And "Let me clarify" means "You completely misunderstood my last email!"

Of course, we have come a long way since 1904, when people still communicated regularly through written letters and legalizing divorce had become a hot topic in Spain. Carmen de Burgos wrote to many of the famous personalities of the day asking their opinions on the subject. For example, she wrote to Gumersindo de Azcárate, a center-left politician. So what exactly did Azcárate mean when he wrote back the following? "It would have been my pleasure to correspond with you . . . but due to the delicacy of the matter . . . it must be given a close examination, which, for now, would not be possible for me because of my innumerable occupations that leave me overwhelmed with work. I am truly sorry for being unable to satisfy you and would like to take this opportunity to send you my warmest regards." I would love to use this formula one day, but unfortunately, I have not yet found someone I despise this deeply.

But this was written in 1904 Spain, not today, and not in English. I don't think the letter was meant to be sarcastic or rude, though it might seem sarcastic to today's readers. So, as a translator, I have a dilemma. Do I translate this letter in a way that sticks closely to the Spanish text, possibly giving modern readers the impression that it is sarcastic or presumptuous, or do I try to adapt it to make it sound, by today's standards, like a polite but sincere refusal? I think that to accomplish the second approach, the letter would have to be a little less gushy and simultaneously a little less bland.

I don't have a good answer for this question, but I translated Azcárate's response in a way that sticks closely to the Spanish text because I have a vague sense that readers will understand, without the need for any added explanation, that this letter was written in a different time and place, and they will interpret it accordingly. Interestingly, almost all the politicians represented in this book (as opposed to the writers and other celebrities) wrote similar letters. Thus, I think the real translation of this letter is "I am a politician, and your issue is too toxic for me."

Speaking of styles, there are slight differences in how valedictions are used in the United States and the United Kingdom. For example, I'm told that, for writers in the United Kingdom, the valediction "Best" sounds somewhat curt, and they prefer "Best regards." British English also uses "Yours sincerely" and "Yours faithfully," whereas writers of English in the United States prefer "Sincerely" or even "Yours truly." There are national preferences and there are personal preferences. Some might consider "Cordially" or "Respectfully" to be a nice way to end, but others think these terms sound cold.

But whatever the differences between English in the United Kingdom and the United States, the differences between English and Spanish from one century ago are clearly much greater. Even today, Spanish tolerates much longer, and more intricate, more decorous, sentences. But especially back then, closings were often longer and more involved—much more involved.

An example of a middle-of-the-road closing is the one used by the same politician above: *de usted muy seguro servidor que besa sus pies.* Literally translated, this would be, roughly, "your very trusty servant that kisses your feet." But this is just a standard closing. I chose to translate it as "I send you my warmest regards." Spanish closings can be up to two or three lines long, but they are routinely translated into English as "Sincerely." My translation is a compromise. It gives a slight intimation of the Spanish, but it also communicates that it is standard.

Nevertheless, there is some variation in closing phrases. The below list shows some examples and ranks them by their degree of perceived warmth in English and Spanish. Granted, this list is subjective and arbitrary. The Spanish is followed by what some people call a literal translation and by my preferred translation; in one case the two translations are the same:

besa sus pies
kiss your feet
Sincerely

de usted muy seguro servidor q. b. s. p. (*"que besa sus pies,"* abbreviated)
your very trusty servant t. k. y. f. ("that kisses your feet," abbreviated)
Warmest regards

de usted atento s. s. q. b. s. p. (*"seguro servidor que besa sus pies,"* abbreviated)
courteously, your t. s. t. k. y. f. ("trusty servant that kisses your feet," abbreviated)
Respectfully yours

de usted respetuosamente servidor y amigo q. b. s. p.
respectfully, your servant and friend t. k. y. f.
Respectfully yours, your friend

su amigo y admirador q. l. b. l. p. (*"que le besa los pies,"*
   a variation on "que besa sus pies");
your friend and admirer t. k. y. f.
Your friend and admirer

de usted muy afectísimo y respetuoso compañero que besa sus pies
your extremely affectionate and respectful *compañero* that
   kisses your feet
Very, very respectfully yours

de usted humilde compañero y lector
your humble *compañero* and reader

siempre suyo afectísimo amigo
always your very affectionate friend
Very truly yours

*En este soliloquio encontrará usted siempre, siempre, siempre a
   su rendido servidor y apasionado* [name]
In this soliloquy you will always, always, always find your
   surrendered servant and impassioned [name]
Very, very truly yours, from your true and impassioned
   admirer

*Rogando a usted me ponga a los pies de la muy distinguida
   escritora Doña Carmen de Burgos Seguí, se le ofrece muy
   afectísimo admirador, que besa los suyos*
Begging you to put me at the feet of the most
   distinguished writer Doña Carmen de Burgos Seguí, I
   offer you an extremely affectionate admirer that kisses
   your feet
Very, very truly yours, Doña Carmen de Burgos Seguí,
   distinguished writer. Your very affectionate admirer

   This custom of foot and hand kissing originated in Persia
during the Achaemenid Empire and was brought to Europe
by Alexander the Great. During the Roman Empire, it became common to kiss the emperor's feet and the hem of his

purple robe as a sign of loyalty and respect. Pope John I was the first pope to have his feet kissed, but the custom was made official Catholic tradition by Pope Constantine I in 709 CE. While this tradition predates Christianity, the justification for it was the story of a woman sinner who kissed the feet of Jesus (Luke 7.36–50). The practice was done away with in the 1950s by Pope John XXIII, although hand kissing as a sign of veneration still persisted. In 2019, Pope Francis created controversy within the Catholic Church by appearing to evade having his ring kissed. Little by little, it appears that the Church is moving away from this tradition.

The custom of referring to oneself as a servant or slave when closing a letter is common in many Romance languages. The Italian word *ciao* comes from *schiavo*, or "slave." "Thank you" in Portuguese is *obrigado* or *obrigada*, meaning "obliged" (as in a servant or indebted person). "Much obliged" is probably the closest thing English has to this formula. Nowadays, it is common throughout the Spanish-speaking world to end an informal letter simply with *un beso* or *besos* ("a kiss" or "kisses"). But although *besos* may seem much less servile than the Spanish closings listed above, those older closings would not have sounded servile to an early-twentieth-century Spaniard. Maybe they sounded like "much obliged."

Any written work is a form of communication between a writer and a reader. Readers, especially today's readers of emails and text messages, often read into things in a certain way. The nicest person on the planet may inadvertently sound angry online. But readers in early-twentieth-century Spain would have read into things in a different way. My job as a translator is, ultimately, to try to put myself in the shoes of the various writers and communicate their thoughts in a different language, time, and place. But as a reader, your job is also to try put yourself into the shoes of another kind of reader, to "self-transport," if you will, to that time and place, to read through someone else's eyes.

Can you imagine a world where divorce was illegal? Where a person was expected to get married once and only once? Where many believed a person should never get divorced or remarried for any reason? Even if the husband turns out to be an alcoholic who beats his wife? Even if he dies? Imagine a world without the Internet or television, where a letter to the editor is something riveting that everyone reads and discusses. Imagine a world where much of what we consider basic science is completely new, where chemical bonds are not yet fully understood (marriage bonds and chemical bonds are compared a number of times in *Divorce in Spain*).

In short, these letters represent one of the main ways that people communicated in early twentieth-century Spain. The ideas in the letters collected in *Divorce in Spain* were completely modern at the time—and for many, they were also completely new. There is a sense of danger and excitement in these letters. The people who wrote them were the most important celebrities of the day. Literate people would have read these letters and then discussed them with their friends, the way we might discuss the latest *Netflix* miniseries. *"Can you believe what so-and-so wrote about divorce? He compared it to chemical affinities!" "Scandalous! What exactly are chemical affinities?"*

For the convenience of readers, Rebecca Bender provides background information on the letters, and I discuss language matters, in numbered footnotes to the translation; my notes, being fewer, are labeled "Translator's note." Burgos's three footnotes from the original edition of *Divorce in Spain* are marked with asterisks. I consulted the Royal Spanish Academy's extensive dictionary in translating certain terms.

SF

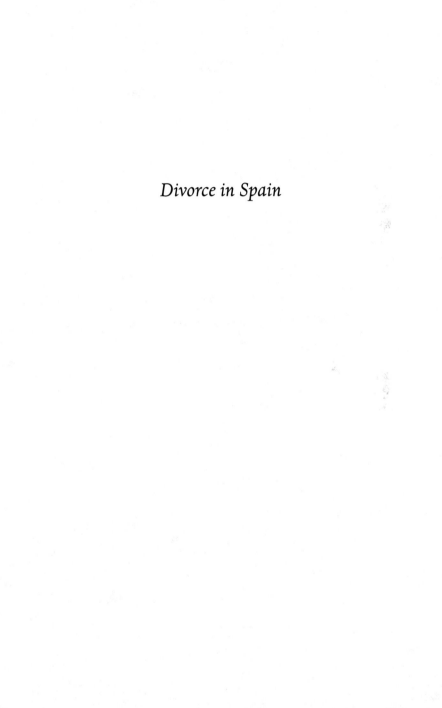

Divorce in Spain

DEAR READER

It is an old custom of ours to explain to the reader, whether they be curious or indifferent, the origin and object of the work we place in their hands, although we don't necessarily tell them the truth.

One person who dreams of glory declares they are publishing their books for mere spiritual expansion, and another whose aim is to make money tries to pass themselves off as disdainful of profit.

This book was born by chance, as is the case with most things thought to be intentional.

While searching for something fresh for my daily column in *Diario Universal*, I ran across a letter signed by a notable writer and esteemed friend, Don Vicente Casanova, who urged me to give the news regarding the formation of a Club of Unhappily Married Couples.

The notice appeared in the newspaper without any thought as to how it might be received. It became worthy enough to catch the attention of a señora with the initials C. V. de P., who sent in a well-written letter that I rushed to print, giving rise to the others that followed.

The idea of divorce "has fallen among the señoras like May showers on land thirsty for beneficent rain," is more or less what my colleague Durante wrote in the beautiful piece published at the beginning of the plebiscite; although it was not just among the señoras—the entire nation perceived an agreeable echo when it heard this idea articulated. Divorce is one of the many social issues that must be discussed without fear of the *"anathema sit."*[1]

Readers of our newspaper, men and women, sent in such an abundance of opinions that the dictates against repetition and a lack of space prevented me from being able to include all of them, as I would have liked to do.

I wanted to learn the opinions of eminent men—and writers, those champions of progress, heeded my call in such a way as to make me truly grateful.

I was less fortunate when it came to learning the opinions of politicians.

Their ideas often tend to change, and the issue of divorce threatens to pass from the columns of the newspaper to Parliament. Doubtless, they were scared of jeopardizing themselves, and very few stated their way of thinking.

With complete impartiality, we have printed what was said to us in favor and against divorce, and we have even included notes from those who declined to give an opinion, to show that we did want to include people of all ways of thinking and from every political party.

----

1. Latin for "Let him be anathema." A formal Church pronouncement said when the Church formally rejects a doctrine or holders of a doctrine: that is, in an excommunication.

Out of a desire to record for perpetuity the first steps toward the establishment of this societal improvement, we are impelled to compile all that was said in the plebiscite in one volume, so that these letters will not be lost to the dizzying speed of the newspaper page and so that they may be a seed of progress thrown to the wind, which one day will germinate.

Up to now, the book has been a reflection of one soul, one mind. It is a test of the book *Collective or Social*, very apropos to the spirit of our times.[2] The signatures that grace these pages enrich the soil for that seed of progress with the humility of those who have shared their ideas with us.

COLOMBINE

---

2. *Translator's note.* While it is unclear what book Burgos is referring to, her statement is about universal consciousness, a widely used concept at the time that was a precursor to Carl Jung's term *collective unconscious*. The idea was that each letter in the book was a separate, even contradictory entity, but as a whole the letters represented Spanish society as one universal consciousness.

Readings for Women (Miscellany)

I have been assured that in a very short while, a "Club of Unhappily Married Couples" will be formed in Madrid so that these couples can express their grievances and study the issue in all its aspects, drawing up the basis for a divorce law that they intend to submit to the legislative chambers.

Notice in *Diario Universal*, 20 December 1903,
which gave rise to this plebiscite

Señora Colombine:

Should we or should we not institute divorce in Spain?
No, and a thousand times no, not in Spain or anywhere
else, and in Spain less than anywhere else.

Back when I used to write verse, D. Teodoro Guerrero
asked me to write some quatrains for his famous and extremely witty *Trial of Marriage*, and so I sent him these
and other quintets in which my opinion may be found in
condensed form and which, because they refer to remarriage, are also applicable to divorce:

> And also, with what right
> may he who swore eternal love
> judge that the bond be unmade
> and profane the holy bed
> that his wife did consecrate?
> Never can death
> kill love, and to its glory
> man must always raise
> in his chest an altar
> to venerate its memory.

That was what I thought in 1884, and I still think this way. And if remarriage seems to me to be wrong, what do *you* think I think about divorce?

There are many marriages in which there is no love whatsoever! I know that; for these people, I would accept divorce less than for others, as punishment for their disgrace, selfishness, and ignorance.

I have neither the time nor the space to enter into lengthy disquisitions, nor do I believe I am being asked for more than a personal impression regarding a matter that has been so debated in books, journals, newspapers, novels, the theater, and Parliament.

I am the sworn enemy of divorce, whether the matter is examined from a moral or sociological perspective, with respect to its artistic aspect or its social significance. And in Spain especially, with our impressionistic idiosyncrasy and our southern temperament, I firmly believe that the establishment of divorce would be an extremely grave ill of incalculable import.

If for many their marriage is not going well . . . let them grin and bear it! It will still serve as a beneficial, living lesson for others who wish to get married, and their example, if it is well studied, will allow those who take seriously the worthy task of starting a new family to come to enlightening deductions and rules of conduct.

No matter how much harm could be caused by the indissolubility of the marriage bond, it could never be as much as that caused by the establishment of divorce.

You, a distinguished writer who lowers herself to my level to ask my opinion, believe me: let's leave things as they are . . . leave well enough alone!

FERNANDO ARAUJO[3]

Señora Colombine:

My dear madam, it would have been my pleasure to correspond with you at your invitation on the subject of divorce, but due to the delicacy of the matter, and also its newness for our public, it must be given a close examination, which, for now, would not be possible for me because of my innumerable occupations that leave me overwhelmed with work.

I am truly sorry for being unable to satisfy you and would like to take this opportunity to send you my warmest regards,

GUMERSINDO DE AZCÁRATE[4]

---

3. Fernando Ricardo Araujo y Gómez was a journalist and professor of French. He was an adherent of Krausism, an idealist philosophy that valued justice and progressive issues like education reform and that was quite popular in Spain during the late nineteenth century. Krausism heavily influenced Burgos's education and progressive thinking.

4. Gumersindo de Azcárate was a jurist and Krausist politician.

Señora Colombine:

Dear madam, it is very kind of you to ask my opinion on divorce.

I am a firm supporter of this social reform. Do I believe there to be so much adultery in Spain that divorce is necessary?

No, that is not what I believe. What's more, if we were able to obtain statistics on adultery in Spain, I am certain that the number, in comparison with the numbers in other European countries, would be insignificant.

Does this point to our great morality? No. Rather, there is no zest for life, a lack of passion.

Regardless of what anyone says, Spain is the coldest and least passionate country in Europe. There is the legend, that's true, that we Spanish men are terrible and that Spanish women are fiery and with a volcanic heart. What more could a man possibly want!

No matter how sad it may be, we must admit that we are a sickly and weak people, cruel and without strong passions. The blood of the lavish, intelligent, and cold Semite courses through the veins of almost every Spaniard. And like those of the Moors, our love lives are scant, and the love lives of women and residents in our provincial capitals are nil.[5]

---

5. *Semite* is a term for Jews and Arabs, as well as other groups of Middle Eastern origin, but in this passage the writer seems to use *Semites* and *Moors* interchangeably to mean North African Muslims.

In Spain, men and women live as if they belonged to a different species; they speak to each other through a thick veil of considerations and formulas.

Men say they cannot talk to women because their conversation is nothing but fabric-store conversation, but I have heard some señoritas say that they cannot talk to men because of how stupid they are.

I don't know who is right. The fact is that this lack of relations between the sexes, as well as the shortage of passion, makes for little enthusiasm between men and women, whether married or single.

The result: there is very little adultery, and so there is not much practical use for divorce.

There is one other thing. If divorce were established in Spain in cases of adultery, the same thing would happen as occurred with civil marriage—the institution would be destroyed, and it would become an institution without life, like an instrument with no use, like a microscope in the hands of a savage.

If I believe that divorce has no practical value, why do I support it? I support it because anything that breaks through this scab of laws, precepts, customs, and intangible and immutable dogmas, which do not allow us to live, seems like a good thing to me.

I support it because I believe we must declare that everything is revocable, nothing is definitive, and everything can transform and improve.

Against this progressive idea is a Catholic sentiment of immutability, of doctrine and dogma, which is held as much by those of us who call themselves advanced as by those who consider themselves reactionary, as much by Salmerón as by Nocedal, by Unamuno as by Father Coloma.

We are subject to so many laws and precepts, so much order, that we have been destroyed by the dominion of the code—of morals, society, and appearances—that even if divorce is nothing more than a small respite, one less chain to bind us, it is already something.

Raising the issue of divorce can at present have a good effect. Discussion and scandal . . .

If we simply speak of the issue out loud, protests will come from every corner of every sacristy in Spain, from every mystical and worldly congregation, from the theater boxes, from the stage, and even from the brothels.

To scandalize is something. When morality is absurd, scandal can be a form of good morals. I won't continue, so my letter doesn't go on forever.

Respectfully yours,

PÍO BAROJA[6]

---

6. Pío Baroja y Nessi was one of the most important Spanish writers of the Generation of '98. As a young person, Baroja sympathized with anarchism and anticlericalism, but he grew more conservative later in life. He is best known as a novelist and for his 1911 masterpiece *El árbol de la ciencia* (*The Tree of Knowledge*).

When the partners in a married couple do not understand each other, there is constant suffering, which divorce can prevent, but this measure, which is always extreme, is only applicable to those that do not have children—who should not perceive the discord that exists between their parents. If the partners do not love each other as husband and wife, they can still be good upstanding friends and come to agree with each other on the good guidance of their children.

The mother, if she does her duty, will not have time to be bored, and the father, between his work and amusement, will come home tired. And with the affection from the little ones, he surely will come home with pleasure.

VISCOUNTESS OF BARRANTES

Señora Colombine:

I am a staunch supporter of divorce, just like I believe in love and not marriage.

The priest's blessing, the judge's certificate, social conventions—these are human inventions that are laughed at by love, that eternal and whimsical sovereign of the world imagined by every mythology as a fickle and inconstant god.

When love is gone forever, what is the point of trying to maintain the bond of marriage between two people who hate or disdain each other like prisoners attached to the same chain who must satisfy their most indecent necessities together?

Without love, the association between man and woman should not persist, no matter how many blessings sanctify it or laws protect it.

Strong, healthy human beings, when they do not love each other, should say goodbye, without sorrow or bitterness, and take different roads to start again.

VICENTE BLASCO IBÁÑEZ[7]

Divorce of Nuns

A few days ago, we published a telegram from Rome in this newspaper with an account of the important reform that His Holiness Pius X intends to effectuate in the religious orders.

Henceforth, he says, the Catholic Church will not attempt to exert influence on the spirit of novice nuns; only those whose calling has been well proved will take the habit. Also, *vows will not be perpetual and may be dispensed with in cases of regret.*

The news was received by nuns with indescribable joy and demonstrates the cultivated spirit and high-mindedness of Saint Peter's current successor.

---

7. Vicente Blasco Ibáñez was a leftist journalist, republican politician, and important novelist of the Generation of '98. A number of his books were adapted to silent films in Hollywood.

Not all nuns go to the cloister with a true calling, just as not all young women marry for love.

Sometimes an intense mystical feeling, or the allure of this tranquil and mysterious life, or disappointments, sorrows, inexperience, and even selfishness are factors that might lead unwed girls to the convents.

But years pass, and many of these girls become women. The impression that worked on their soul disappears, and regret comes. Why should such a creature be condemned to always suffer the consequences of a momentary lack of foresight?

Nuns call Jesus their *Divine Spouse* and consider themselves *brides of the Lord* on the day they say their vows. They crown their heads with orange blossoms and wear the bridal dress, swearing fidelity to their glorious consort.

It may happen—it does happen—that a worldly love comes to take hold of these innocent hearts, that their lips whisper another name along with their prayers to Christ.

Then these consciences that are darkened by the cloister, these wills that are weakened by fasting, excesses, and sometimes superstitions, believe themselves to be at fault; they *accuse themselves of loving*. They consider something that is a natural law, the most beautiful law in one's life, to be a crime.

Why force upon them an eternal martyrdom? Why make them believe their love is adultery and belittle the idea of God, giving him a weak woman as a wife and a simple mortal as a rival?

Some have not wanted to deal with this logical reasoning. It seems to some that anything concerning religion should remain immutable.

As recorded in the annals of the convents, so many crimes and infractions against religion, violent or otherwise, are born of this mistake.

Today, the supreme leader of the Church is a learned priest. He is as considerate of all human weaknesses as he is severe and virtuous. He understands the deficiencies of some institutions that have been maintained on the basis of rules, and he knows that these institutions have begun to conflict at this point with the organization of a superior society.

If the noble old man accomplishes his work, nuns will be able to go to the convent and kneel before the altar as long as their hearts are pure. If they have regrets, the convent doors are not prison doors, and they can return to the world, get married, be mothers, and worship God while fulfilling the goals of existence.

This can be called *a nun's divorce*, given that it is the end of the spiritual bond that had been considered a mystical marriage and that, in terms of its indissolubility, was equivalent to real marriage.

But if divorcing the *perfect spouse* is permitted, what reason is there to forbid it for the wives of simple mortals? For the children? This issue can be resolved with laws to ensure their welfare.

It would be irreverent to try to penetrate the thoughts of the Holy Father on this matter, which is more sociological than religious, but I am almost sure that someone who opens the cloister door in the name of morals would not allow—in the name of these same morals—the torments, deception, and bad example that is introduced into homes by insisting that human beings live together when they stop loving each other and then wind up hating each other.

CARMEN DE BURGOS

Señora Colombine:

My distinguished friend, with some delay, much to my regret, I am responding to your courteous and reiterated invitation to say what I think about divorce. I will be brief.

The Church, using a barbaric and medieval criterion, only allows divorce when the *ex capite impotentia*[8] has been proved for one of the spouses, as Father Sánchez discusses in his work *On Marriage*.

No moral reason exists that would be enough to justify the rupture of the marriage bond. The Church—with Nature being its accomplice in this regard since it cares only about perpetuating the species—does not concern itself with our happiness. As long as we do not violate its canonical decrees, that is enough. Now since our inner

8. Latin for "arising from impotence."

peace is over and above the unavoidable egoism of nature and Church orthodoxies, the law should be hospitable to the unfortunate men and women who want to separate. Maintaining a bond that would be broken without these shackles is criminal.

Many of our misfortunes are due to the fact that the dissonance of character of our parents continues to have repercussions on our psyches. Divorce is healthy and moral. At minimum it should be instituted here so that certain men don't become too big-headed with their ignominies.

Respectfully yours, your friend,

MANUEL BUENO[9]

Señora Colombine:

Dear distinguished madam, indeed, it was not until the 20th that I had the honor of receiving the letter from you, whose work I have read closely and with the attention it deserves. The matter you pose is of the utmost importance and requires close study. I will aim to send you

---

9. Manuel Bueno Bengoechea was a journalist, theater critic, and novelist who is sometimes included in the Generation of '98. At the end of the nineteenth century, he became active in the Socialist Association of Bilbao and the General Union of Workers, a trade union associated with the Spanish Socialist Workers' Party. By the 1920s, however, he came to support the dictatorship of Miguel Primo de Rivera. He died at the hands of the Republican Army at the onset of the Spanish Civil War in 1936.

a few quatrains before the date you indicated, or in any case I will definitely do it at some point in the future.

Respectfully,

JOSÉ CANALEJAS

Señora Colombine:

Señora and very distinguished friend: Due to the fact that I go to the offices of *Nuevo Mundo* very seldom and due to being away from Madrid, I did not receive your gracious inquiry on the establishment of divorce in Spain until yesterday. It is long since past the deadline for responses, but I don't want my very brief one to be left out—if due to its lateness, it cannot be published, I hope it has arrived in time to prove to you my respect and consideration.

The question to me is extremely simple. In the painful realities of our lives, does divorce exist among us? Without a doubt; there is no one who is unaware of the abundant examples of marriages broken up by that lack of love that follows disillusionment or disappointment. So if the laws are meant to respond to the necessities of life, how is it that the establishment of divorce is not essential in Spain?

I very clearly understand the extremely serious disadvantages of this reform. Our lack of consciousness and foresight, our incredible intellectual and moral backwardness, our general situation of human suffering—and

I won't mention the connection between one thing and the other or all these things with our current problem, trusting that such a perspicacious reader as yourself can do that on your own—these things would mean that a few years after the establishment of divorce, half of Spanish women who are no longer single but not yet widowed would be divorced, with all the concomitant problems of this status in a society like ours, which is so unaccustomed to respecting women, and without any of the advantages of manumission and independence, which our society would make illusory, if not the basis of a new and more ignominious slavery.

There you have the obverse and the reverse of my thinking. I would write an entire book with pleasure—of course, forgetting about the readers—to lay out the reasoning for one thing and the other and to tease from one thing and the other a definitive statement that could be synthesized thus: let divorce become law, since in reality it already is, but with all the precautions compelled by the fear that the people who get married so thoughtlessly will divorce just as thoughtlessly; and above all, let it become law at the same time as all those laws, and especially with all the necessary social education, that—in consideration of the Spanish pedagogical and economic problems—deal head-on with solving the arduous and distressing problem of the Spanish woman, the most beautiful in the world, and the unhappiest in Western civilization.

And now that I know who "Colombine" is in *Diario Universal*, I send you extremely cordial congratulations for honoring a pseudonym that the admirable reporter Henry Fouquier made glorious a few years ago in *L'écho de Paris.* Very sincerely yours,

SALVADOR CANALS[10]

Divorce

I haven't been able to follow step-by-step the information published in a fellow newspaper from Madrid by the distinguished woman writer who hides her name under the pseudonym Colombine. I haven't been able to, and I'm sorry about that. Without a doubt, regarding the dreadful issue, many good things and many new things, and maybe even some things that were both good and new, must have been set forth there. Reduced to the isolated inspiration of my intellect, I fear that what I have to say on the topic is deserving of the famous words of a biting art critic: the new things are not good, and the good things are not new.[11]

---

10. Salvador Canals y Vilaró was born in Puerto Rico and moved to Spain at the age of eighteen, where he first worked as a journalist. In 1902 he was appointed press secretary by the conservative Antonio Maura, and in 1903 he was elected to the Spanish Parliament as a Conservative deputy.

11. Calderón is referring to an exchange between Christoph Friedrich Nicolai and Gotthold Ephraim Lessing in which Nicolai challenged Lessing: "You must admit that Voltaire has lately said many new and good things." "Certainly," Lessing responded, "but the new things are not good, and the good things are not new." Lessing, *Nathan the Wise: A Dramatic Poem*, translated by Ellen Frothingham, Henry Holt, 1873, p. xv.

The first thing we have to do before addressing the issue is discard our religious prejudice. Without this precaution, there is no way to make ourselves understood. Once a person asserts that marriage is a sacrament, there is no longer any way to know what marriage really is. What is the point of arguing with those that will not argue? Let them continue eternally repeating their eternal aphorism: *quos Deus conjunvit homini non separent.*[12]

And once we have done that, if we want to address the issue, we find ourselves, surprisingly, with the fact that such an issue does not exist. Because, to sum it up, what is marriage? A contract? A religious ceremony consecrated by the priest's blessing? A civil ceremony sanctioned by the proper authorities? These are forms, rituals. According to Roman legal experts, marriage is the union of a man and a woman in an indivisible partnership. According to modern ones, marriage is a union between a man and a woman, of such absolute intimacy that it forms between them something like a single personality in common.

While marriage so understood does persist, it is said that there is no divorce. As soon as marriage so understood ceases to exist, divorce becomes necessary—no matter what the priest, the judge, the legislator, or society may say. It all boils down to this truism: divorce is a problem that disappears as soon as we touch it.

Measures to put into effect the rights and responsibilities that emanate from the frustrated marriage? Restric-

---

12. "What God has joined together, let no man separate"; Matt. 19.6.

tions aiming to prevent the marriage from being dissolved with the same despicable flippancy with which it was performed? Precautions to ensure that divorce does not make marriage an instrument of licentiousness? Legal guarantees for the rights of women and for the present and future of the children? Congratulations. But that is all a different kettle of fish. These are all problems that derive from divorce; they are not the problem of divorce. Regarding divorce, I consider the observation of my dear friend Álvaro de Albornoz to be definitive. Divorce is a fact. Let everyone consult their own experience and say they have not known or do not know apparent marriages that are actually nothing of the sort, cold homes, sullied unions, spouses who are tied to their yoke and whose existence is a living hell.

Faced with this painful reality, what should the government and society do? Ignore it? Deny it? Sweep it under the rug with laws or customary conventionalisms? Proclaim the existence of what doesn't exist and the effectiveness of a ghost? Turn our entire lives into an endless atonement for one day's mistake? Declare the mistake irremediable and the straying irredeemable? Transform the holy matrimonial union into an involuntary chain? Forever close the path of rehabilitation and the road of happiness to those who have erred? Turn the fantasy of happiness into an instrument of torture and call hell paradise? To defend the realm of woman condemn her to unhappiness for the rest of her life? Look after the interests of children by forcing them to bear witness to the conflicts of their parents? Invert the relationship between the law and life, subjugating reality to fiction and replacing the truth with appearances?

Chance determines that two people of the opposite sex meet one day. They are born and raised in different environments, and they have dissimilar ideas, feelings, customs, beliefs, likes, manias. If mere passion is what attracts them—what risk of error, disappointment, disillusionment, aggravation! If it is calculation—how wretched and blind is he who is driven by such sordid interests! The courtship is a dramatic comedy in which each of the actors plays a role. Among Latin peoples—whose degree of mistrust is proportional to the measure of their virtue— the relationship between the sexes is, rather than one of frankness and expansion, one of suspicion and hostility. The bride and groom join together without knowing one another. Every honeymoon is an exploration, a voyage of discovery. The Church, such an enemy of the breaking of the marriage bond, requires only the couple's consent to bind them. The State, so solicitous when it come to the rights and welfare of the children, doesn't think to find out whether the couple is even capable of raising strong, healthy children. Where the doctor should intervene, the priest does. And so with such thoughtless levity, the most transcendent ceremony in life is reduced to the most ordinary. And the Church and State want this bond contracted in this way to be indissoluble and for life!

Arguing in favor of the establishment of divorce is pure common sense. A law that authorizes divorce does not force anyone to get divorced. In this we find the excellence of the so-called permissive laws (some more or some less deserving of the name). Much as legislators must be sparing in enacting measures that require coercion, they must also be expansive and liberal when it comes to measures that only apply at the request of the interested parties. And if the divorce law is not taken advantage of? If centuries go by, as in ancient Rome, without anyone bringing an action of this sort? All the better: the law remains without application, though it may be used one day. As for those that do not wish to divorce, curse them if the divorce law disturbs them. A single case, just one, in which divorce is logical, legitimate, and redemptive is enough to justify its existence and demonstrate the utility of such a law. And is there anyone who dares deny that such a case may exist?

Two opposing prejudices stand in the way of this and other social problems. Simple ultraradicalism is inclined to regard the current institutions as organizations engendered by artifice and sinister motives to the benefit of the privileged. So it is not unusual to find men of simple mentality who, praising, for example, free love, are amazed that something they find so natural has never been sanctioned by any state. Extreme conservatism fails to understand any institutions other than those they can see before their very eyes, and, making of the current ephemeral reality everlasting law for life, they tremble over the future of human society the moment a transformation of the present order looms on the horizon. The conservative also tends to take as positive truth the falsity of official conventions. Self-restraint outside marriage, monogamy, indissoluble unions—they would all be very nice if not for the existence of seduction, adultery, and especially prostitution, a disgraceful blot on society and the species. Regardless of what the *legal truth* is, such deviations constitute, for the most part, the current relations between the sexes.

It is important to rectify both errors. We must proclaim, against the one, that not only has the present constitution of the family been, and continues to be, in part, the best that it can be, or, if you will, the least bad that it can be, within the physical, climatic, ethnic, historical, social, and economic conditions in which it was engendered—but also that this constitution of the family is the only one possible. Against the other side, we must demonstrate that the organization of the family unit, far from being immutable, has evolved continuously throughout the course of time and that all changes in the conditions of life inevitably affect the constitution of the family, whether lawmakers like it or not. The intellectual, social, and economic emancipation of women, which feminism strives for, allows us to envision in the future a profound transformation of reciprocal relations between the sexes.

ALFREDO CALDERÓN[13]
(from *La Publicidad*, Barcelona)

---

13. Alfredo Calderón y Arana was a republican journalist and writer as well as an adherent of Krausism.

Let's Talk about Divorce

These days the *Divorce Question* has been making the rounds of Madrid newspapers, like a ball, ever since *Diario Universal* threw into the present state of things Colombine, a pseudonym behind which hides a very illustrious, pleasant, and indefatigable woman journalist.

Many writers of both sexes have given the issue their two cents, some with more, some with less force, some hitting the target right on the nose, others less so. On balance, we can infer from the opinions published that the proponents of divorce will come out victorious.

To me, the game has been theirs ever since the world came into existence—ever since men and women have existed.

Ever since love has been posited as a fundamental principle of humanity whereby human beings of different sexes join together and engender the races. It has been posited in the same way as every principle ruled by Nature and can disappear only if Nature disappears.

Any effort by civilizations to reform these principles of Nature, to say nothing of abolishing them completely, would be useless; thus, the most powerful magnate may mobilize all his armies on land and sea, and turn all his ministries upside down, but he cannot cause the sun to stop for a moment over his lands.

They say Joshua achieved such a mercy so he could finish a battle. That is possible. Back then, the sun was very unoccupied because a large portion of the earth was un-inhabited; there wasn't such demand for heat and light as there is today, and the sun could allow itself the luxury of giving its beneficiaries a small gratuity.

But today that would have been impossible for Joshua; the sun's dynamos are insufficient for it to be able to illuminate us for as long as our work requires, and so it has given way to electrical power plants, which in vain try to compete with it.

But the sun does not have accountants. The *law of gravity* does not figure into our Constitution, even if it is one of the gravest (nor has there been, to my knowledge, any proposal to that end in Parliament); nevertheless, Maura can already parade every Civil Guard division through the streets, and Sánchez Guerra[14] (whose name they are calling for in El Paseo de Areneros) can put sand down for the horses[15]—this is their way of doing more cavalry charges against the taxpayers—but they cannot stop rocks from falling to the ground when they have been thrown into the air. It is just as impossible, if not more so, to prevent two human beings who love each other from joining together.

---

14. Antonio Maura Montaner was a Liberal delegate in Parliament who switched to the Conservative Party in 1903. Between 1902 and 1903 he carried out a series of police reforms. In December 1903 (around the time of this letter), Maura became prime minister, and José Sánchez Guerra y Martínez became minister of the interior.

15. There is wordplay here between the Spanish term *enarenar* ("sand") and the name of the street El Paseo de Areneros ("Boulevard of the Areneros"). An *arenero* is a person responsible for the sand in a bullring.

The only thing Maura can do, as he has done many times, is downplay the importance of falling rocks and say that there were only a few tiny ones and that they were thrown by kids, which is exactly what society does with unions that do not conform to legislation regarding individuals: downplay their importance and deny them any rights.

But the unions of people who love each other will always continue to exist, with or without society's permission, just as rocks will always continue to fall due to gravity, with or without Maura's permission.

I refer to the testimony of parents who lost custody of their daughters, or whose daughters had surprise marriages or were simply stolen from them, as Don Juan stole the daughter of the imbecile Comendador. I mean, the imbecile in this drama is the mother superior.[16]

When two lovers want to join together, the only two options are to kill them or let them be. The majority of parents opt for the latter after having exhausted their entire repertoire of punishments, threats of disinheriting, and even curses.

A relationship between princes and peasants and princesses and peasants is a child's fairy tale that sometimes people do enjoy in reality.

---

16. Referring to the 1844 play *Don Juan Tenorio*, written by José Zorrilla, which portrays Don Juan as a depraved womanizer. The Comendador, a respected member of the elite classes, sends his daughter to a convent to protect her, only for Don Juan to outsmart the mother superior and seduce the Comendador's daughter anyway.

The catchphrase *Let them be buried together* was devised in a newsroom, like all the usual section headings.

"Naturally, love is a fundamental principle of Nature, just like heat and light," exclaim those who are not in favor of divorce.

Well, *cogite, cogite*,[17] as the schoolmasters of antiquity used to say when they had caught their disciples in a trap.

If you admit that human beings join together by natural law, that they fall like rocks, as the sun gives light and heats us, then you have no choice but to admit that they also separate, just as there is night and cold.

Because divorce is to marriage, or wedlock, or whatever you want to call it, as night is to day, as winter is to the dog days of summer, as the identity card of Nozaleda[18] is to the salary afforded him in the budget.

To accept that love is inevitable without also accepting that divorce is inevitable is like accepting the day while denying the night, like accepting the existence of the equator while denying the poles, like accepting the *congrua portio* without paying for the identity card.[19]

---

17. Latin for "think, think."

18. In the so-called *caso Nozaleda* ("Nozaleda case"), which was in the news roughly at the same time as this plebiscite, the conservative minister Antonio Maura named Bernardino Nozaleda the archbishop of Valencia. The liberal newspapers of the day opposed this appointment. They claimed that Nozaleda was anti-Spanish because he had been archbishop of Manila. Among other things, they said he no longer had Spanish citizenship (hence no Spanish identity card).

19. The *congrua portio* is a cleric's yearly income.

Now, as always, when a man and a woman cannot resist leaving each other, either they give each other tacit permission to do what they want (divorce by sainete[20]), they give each other express permission through amicable separation (divorce by comedy), or he shoots her or she gives him a poison tea (divorce by drama).

Look at our theater, a mirror of our lives. We see that couples have been coming together and breaking up at will before the invention of the divorce law, just as days and nights followed each other before the invention of calendars and clocks, just as hot and cold existed before the creation of thermometers.

It could get on Mother Nature's nerves if she were forced to be subject to the laws of men; it would be nice if it didn't rain until it was authorized by a decree in the *Gazette*.

Well, I think the legal question of divorce is like clockwork; we don't yet have divorce because everything comes to Spain a century behind, just like clocks and thermometers.

And I think that since it's purely a question of timing, it is only of interest to a tiny fraction of society, to those who allow themselves the luxury of possessing a fortune. As for those who don't have to worry about dividing their estates—like hell do they need a legal mechanism to separate.

---

20. A humorous one-act play.

"But the children?" they say. Ay! When the parents don't love each other, with or without divorce, the children, regardless of their class, are left in the worst possible situation.

Oh sure, let them stay together for the good of the children!

EL SASTRE DEL CAMPILLO[21]
(from *El Liberal*)

Señora Colombine:

My distinguished friend: I just finished reading an admirable book. The book is titled *Life of the Reverend Mother Du Rousier, Founder of the Religious of the Sacred Heart in Chile*. Upon finishing this beautiful book, I took a moment to meditate on the life of these nuns, the peaceful and resigned life of these nuns who forswear humanly love to devote themselves to religious contemplation, to mystic exaltation . . . And haven't I also thought about those two nice nuns, the two sisters who wanted—recently—to cut the distance between them and their beloved Master.

Then I think about how I am to tell you my feelings on divorce, which in every country today is an all-consuming preoccupation by whose heat the most beautiful flowers

---

21. Pseudonym for Antonio Martínez Viérgol, a playwright, poet, and journalist.

of artistry have blossomed—from *Anna Karenina* to *When We Dead Awaken*, *Le dédale* and *L'adversaire*, and in a certain way, these other works of pure, exquisite art in which there is a victim of love, a beautiful victim immolated on the altar of love: *The Dead City* and *Aglavaine and Selysette*, as well as the supreme poem of the supreme Spanish dramatic poet, *Sacrificios*.[22]

And here's my insignificant opinion: To me there's nothing more sacred than love. How many mysteries are locked away in that word? In love, as in chemistry, everything is a matter of elective affinities. That means we have no right to demand that love last forever. It will last as long as a third element capable of forming a more stable combination with one of the other two does not step in. In this case, protesting is out of the question. The element that remains isolated can go off in search of another free or divorced element with whom to form a pleasant association and with whom to reflect on the fickleness of mundane vanities or the absolute dominion of Nature, which imposes its laws so inescapably. Wasn't that precisely the thesis of one of the novels of the Jupiter of Weimar?[23] And doesn't all this mean that what is amorous attraction and what is instinctive or emotional struggle seem to me fair and natural? Divorce is a logical consequence of the laws

---

22. Referring, respectively, to works by Leo Tolstoy, Henrik Ibsen, Paul Hervieu (*The Labyrinth*), Alfred Capus and Emmanuel Arène (*The Adversary*), Gabriele D'Annunzio, Maurice Maeterlink, and Jacinto Benavente y Martínez (*Sacrifices*).

23. *The Sorrows of Young Werther* (1774), by Johann Wolfgang von Goethe.

governing the universe, and I who am but a "small-time" moralist and aficionado of biology believe myself to have seen all these matters that we are so deeply concerned with today justified in the petty lives of inferior beings, and even in the lives and the *feelings* of atoms—as the author of *Raw Matter and Living Material* would say.[24]

It is true that emotional strife produces horrid malaise in us, but do we know the malaise, the pain, the private suffering of an atom when it combines with another, or when it separates from another with which it has coexisted a long time?

Distinguished friend, I have here a situation for which we small-time biologists use the sweet term *epiphenomena*.

So, dear Colombine, I am in favor of divorce and a modest enemy of Jesuit hypocrisy, and know that I have carefully read—I read everything—a huge number of little handbooks and devotional books that seem to be written to turn great love and great religious feeling into false love and ridiculous feelings.

Your friend and admirer,

BERNARDO G. DE CANDAMO[25]

---

24. *La matière brute et la matière vivant: Étude sur l'origine de la vie et de la mort* (*Raw Matter and Living Matter: A Study on the Origin of Life and Death*), published in 1887 by Joseph Delboeuf.

25. Bernardo G. de Candamo was a journalist, writer, and literature and theater critic belonging to the Generation of '98. He was active in the scientific, literary, and artistic gatherings in the Madrid Athenaeum, and during the Spanish Civil War he saved its library from destruction. After the war, he was blacklisted by the Franco regime but continued writing under a pseudonym.

I accept as my conviction
that marriage shan't be mandatory,
and divorce so very voluntary
(with only one condition):
the child, boy or girl,
of such a union born,
in two equal pieces be torn;
yes, it must be so:
let one half go to the woman,
and the other to the husband be sworn.

LEOPOLDO CANO[26]

If I were married, and if I were extremely happy in my marriage, it would not stop me, Señora Colombine, from responding to your delightful invitation regarding the establishment of divorce in Spain, because in this, as in many things, I do have an opinion.

Let's not argue over whether the Church and the holy fathers have or have not spoken of marriage. Let's not argue if it is a sacrament, a contract, or an institution. Let's see whether it is or isn't beneficial, since in life, we cannot—we should not—ignore what is beneficial.

---

26. Leopoldo Cano was a realist writer, playwright, and military officer. In 1910, he became a member of the Royal Spanish Academy.

35

To live well without hurting anyone is a very holy and very humanitarian doctrine. Do all married couples live well? No. Regarding those couples that do not live well, isn't it fair that they should remedy that? Of course!

Because the following cases are known. A young man and young woman were not happily married, but they found happiness: he with another woman, she with another man. They live happily, but *illegally*. Wouldn't it be better for them to live happily and within the law, given our way of seeing things?

But it is the case that this man has children with his lover, and the woman with her lover. And consequently, while the man's children cannot use their own father's last name, not only do the children of the woman and her lover use her husband's last name, but they must do so. Either that or they won't have a mother . . . officially. This is a monstrosity, isn't it? Well, divorce would end such monstrosities.

Another case, the antithesis of the previous one—everyone knows it. The daughter of Don Carlos of Borbón (the Pretender), Doña Elvira, fell in love with the painter Folchi, who was married, and ran off with him. To avoid *a greater evil*, Pope Leo XIII dissolved the painter's marriage—or *dispensed it*, as they say in the Vatican—so Folchi could marry Doña Elvira. And what about the widow of the living man, you must be wondering? She may also marry whomever she wants.

What has been done with the family of Don Carlos—why can't it be done for other mortals? And even if Rome doesn't want to, why don't the civil authorities?

Don't tell me there is a victim in all this, whether the man or the woman, because victims are the parents whose children are snatched from them *by force* so they can go to war, or the wives whose husbands are taken from them for the same reason, and nobody has thought to abolish wars so as to prevent *victims of separation*.

So you see, Señora Colombine, this is what I think about divorce. You will judge for yourself whether my most humble opinion will be of use to you.

Sincerely,

VICENTE CASANOVA[27]

Dear Friend Colombine:

I am in favor of divorce, and I believe women should be more in favor of it than I am. The indissolubility of marriage harms them more than it harms us men. When he is married, a man scarcely loses his freedom. The woman loses it completely. As long as she does not have more rights and fewer responsibilities, the marriage bond makes her a slave.

<hr />

27. Vicente Casanova y Marzol was a cardinal who became archbishop of Granada in 1921.

Now, if she has more rights, will she have fewer worries? To be clear: if she becomes more of a *citizen*, will she be less fanatical? Because, fine words aside, as long as she sees legal marriage as nothing more than canon law, as long as she believes that to get married one must go to the house of worship and not city hall or the municipal court, speaking to her of divorce is a waste of time.

I insist that women should be the most ardent defenders of this reform because the laws currently in force have forsaken them, both in the civil and canonical realms. One of the legitimate grounds for divorce, according to our legal code, is "adultery of the wife *in any case* and of the husband when it results in public scandal or disparagement." Just like it sounds. For women, in any case, without exception. For men, in no case except public scandal or disparagement. As if there could be adultery of the man without apparent disparagement of his legitimate wife.

Canonical law is more reasonable, considering the adultery of the man to be grounds for divorce in all cases. The nebulousness comes in later, where we see that "the lack of consent by the bride and groom" is grounds for annulment of the marriage, adding that "consent is invalid if it is given by *error*, violence, intimidation, or fraud."

The law refers to error in persona. The letter of the law is clear, but its spirit should refer to other very common mistakes—mistakes made in the real world that the law should address—not only in spirit, but also in letter, as is done in countries where divorce does exist.

In defending his bill in the French Parliament, Alfred Naquet asserted that what women are ignorant of due to their characteristic apathy they will learn as soon as they are informed that men have been given new rights that they too may enjoy. It is true that Naquet was dealing with French women, who have a more open mind than Spanish women.

They say that later Naquet regretted his effort. I am unaware of the veracity of that report. In any case, he could only have regretted putting forward something that any legislator would have done later anyway. His law has destroyed many homes in France. Inaptly destroyed some? Fittingly destroyed others? Well, the good achieved by the latter makes up for the harm done by the former. People talk of those who, because of scandal, have burst into the public sphere. They don't talk of those who, because of their silence, remain unknown. It is well known that twenty people who whisper make more noise than a thousand who keep silent.

"What about the children of the divorced?" they wonder—this is the supreme rationale. I have not seen this issue dealt with more skillfully than in Le berceau, a wonderful comedy by Brieux that has not been translated into Spanish,[28] and I have no idea why because it is much

---

28. *The Cradle*, by Eugène Brieux.

better than *L'adversaire* by Capus and Arène, which our public has misunderstood so thoroughly (and which has been interpreted in such a mediocre way onstage).

Children, if they are not a deterrent to sin, which is almost always the cause of divorce, can be the victims of sin themselves, and in that case maybe it would be better for them to live without a father or a mother than with a father or a mother whose conduct does them much moral harm.

In any case, they may be the reason why the parent who by law is given custody avoids remarriage (which is considered the true disruption of the family), but if that is not the case, this is not a good reason to call divorce bad, since there are widows and widowers who marry and give their children a stepfather or stepmother.

Those who say that where divorce is legal moral corruption triumphs surely forget that in times of intolerance there were also corrupters and depraved people, and licentiousness, adultery, and social crime triumphed then.

Divorce is a sign of progress. Maybe we are not ready for the reform, but the idea is not to blame, we are. Maybe women are more resistant to the reform, but like the author of the French law, I believe that women, by dint of their preservation instinct and their impetus toward noble egoism, will hasten to take advantage of a right that is granted equally to them as to men.

I'm not saying that divorce will only find proponents among those who would readily divorce. No, those who have paradise at home understand how humane and even merciful and kind it would be to put an end to the hell of other homes.

ÁNGEL MARÍA CASTELL[29]

Señora Colombine:

My distinguished good friend: You would like me to give you my opinion on divorce, a red-hot issue today, and, putting into practice the theory that I have often heard you expound in your pleasant and extremely tactful conversation, which is that one should only write what one feels, here is my true and sincere opinion on this very contentious matter, which I *feel* in my heart.

I am not in favor of divorce, because I believe that with the establishment of this reform, we will not manage to cut the root of the evils that this reform *aims* to stop, in other words: we will not prevent the existence of unhappy marriages, nor will we cease to see the sad, grievous scenes of many homes where there does not reign that warmth and good harmony that is born of mutual affection, tolerance, and respect: that which constitutes true happiness in the marital partnership.

On the contrary, I believe this measure would have a counterproductive result. If, knowing what marriage is and knowing what a holy union between two human

---

29. Ángel María Castell was a Basque writer and journalist.

beings is when it is formed through this indissoluble bond, many marriages are made for convenience, for financial gain, or on a whim, or they are imposed on the couple, or made for other reasons that are very far from the noble end that should guide both the woman and the man, it is evident and certain that if we remove from this indissoluble act its import and significance, then couples will more frequently have marriages of this sort, marriages that, as is logical, are sooner or later inclined to fall apart, since between these couples there is no unity of feeling and aspiration, both of which are born from true love, and which *ensure sweet and gentle* happiness, of which fortunately we still see so many edifying examples.

Divorce, that is, giving the husband and wife the facility to undo the holy knot when for some reason it becomes too vexing or unbearable, makes marriage a temporal union, a mere pact or contract that the interested parties may enter into recklessly and without reservation, carried away by their passion or for convenience, and thus our opinion on the desired reform—if it is instituted here, it will aggravate the evil rather than remedy it, and in no way will it resolve the issue that so deeply affects the family in particular and society in general.

The passion with which divorce is demanded and the heatedness with which it is debated demonstrates the increased number of unhappy marriages that exist: these are the voices of egoism that rise up powerfully, demanding a remedy that, while putting an end to the exceptional situation of many marriages, would not yield the desired results, as we believe we have demonstrated.

It follows, in our humble opinion, that marriage should be and surely will continue to be indissoluble; though to avoid, in part, if not fully, the severe discord that affects the peace of families in their homes, marriage should be considered the most important act in life and never a means of speculation, business, or immature satisfaction of one's vanity or whim.

It is mainly up to the man to give the means for this to happen, as long as he has the power to choose (the woman must content herself with the husband fate has given her), and as a deep thinker said, her only *story is marriage.* Despite this big disadvantage, it would be fair to say that women, as a general rule, go to marriage disposed toward abnegation, toward sacrifice, and it is probably often the case that they will not find the happiness their soul ceaselessly aspires to. And so we see her suffering, and she resigns herself to her husband straying or even being disloyal before she would wound the sensitive souls of her children with the sad spectacle of separation.

Nevertheless, no matter how great the abyss that separates two souls in the same home, no matter how inconceivably miserable the two human beings are who live united until death and who hate and repudiate each other so deeply and implacably, the joy given to them by their children and the charms with which they surround the couple's existence are sufficient to counteract all the heartaches produced by marital discord. The love for their children in this case comes to be the sweet balm that smooths the harshness of the most intense sorrows, like a pristine spring that regenerates the spirit, warding away doubt, hate, and fear, like the joyous rays of the sun making their way through the clouds, sweetly illuminating the landscape darkened by heavy clouds.

The sad souls who are incapable of feeling these emotions, who lack the necessary abnegation to sacrifice themselves for the sake of their children, these poor people who, despite finding themselves surrounded by such ineffable joy in their homes, see divorce as the only means of freeing themselves from the yoke of marriage should—it would be strictly just—always live inside the circle of iron in which they voluntarily locked themselves, if for no other reason than as punishment for their lack of foresight or excessive levity, as they were driven to the altar by considerations other than those noble and lofty ones that should guide men when they seek in the love relationship their other half and the means to the highest ends for which they were created.

Nothing more, my charming friend. May this letter serve as public testimony of my affection and admiration for you,

MARÍA DEL PILAR CONTRERAS DE RODRÍGUEZ[30]

---

30. María del Pilar Contreras y Alba de Rodríguez was a prolific writer, poet, composer, and journalist known for her conservative views.

Señora Colombine:

I apologize, dear colleague, for taking so long to answer your kind letter asking my opinion on the topic of divorce.

Other divorces, that of Don Antonio Maura and Spain and that of the dramatic arts and subscription theaters, are to blame.

I believe, as long as there is marriage, divorce is as necessary as quinine, as long as fevers exist. And I think you know what I mean when I say fevers.

Of course, it would be better to eliminate fevers and marriage; we will get there.

While we are getting there, I am, with doctors, for quinine, and with you, for divorce.

Very respectfully yours,

JOAQUÍN DICENTA[31]
5 February 1904

The question is, what do I think about *divorce*? A somewhat difficult question to answer, especially given that I am a single girl whose ideas on this point cannot have

---

31. Joaquín Dicenta Benedicto was a writer, poet, playwright, and journalist. His play *Juan José*, which deals with socialist themes, was one of the most popular plays in Spain before the Civil War, performed yearly on May Day. He was also an avowed atheist and republican politician.

the same depth, nor be expressed with the same clarity, as the ideas of those who have received the marriage blessing, those who know all the ins and outs of married life, who, naturally, can express their ideas on this subject of divorce, which is today such a hot topic of conversation, not only in our country, but especially so outside of it.

To speak to a young girl about divorce is almost like ripping off the rose veil of her illusions, giving her a glimpse of the possibility of such a grave solution, but, well, since this is about my opinion, and since we live in a time when one often hears talk of divorce, such that its existence is not hidden to any of us, I will now discuss it, in accordance with my conscience and using extremely short sentences.

As a devout Catholic, divorce cannot seem to me to be a good thing, since the Church does not allow it and never will: it would be the destruction of the sacrament instituted by our Lord Jesus Christ. I understand that marriage should not be entered into lightly, and only after a mature examination of whether the couple gets along sufficiently and especially whether they *love* each other (although this seems so cliché nowadays) to endure the hardships of this world; but once husband and wife are bound together through this bond imposed by God through the priest, I cannot accept that they may separate under the most trivial pretext, as they can in France, which in my view, constitutes the saddest and most deplorable *advancement* of our century . . .

What God has united cannot be broken apart by man; that is what the Church tells me . . . and I stand by that.

MARÍA DE ECHARRI[32]
Barcelona, 1904

Señora Colombine:

My respected señora and friend: As I was away from Madrid for almost a month, I only today received your letter from the twelfth of this month. I rush to tell you this so that my silence will not be taken for disregard.

In divorce, as in everything, I am at your service, but I should let you know that I am a determined adversary of this unbinding, regardless of what Naquet and the other Jews say.

Is it possible for someone to be in favor of divorce while being an enemy of marriage? There's the rub; I am an enemy to all the sacraments.

But I am your admirer and friend,

NICOLÁS ESTÉVANEZ[33]
23 January 1904

---

32. María de Echarri y Martínez was a Catholic feminist activist and teacher. In 1912, she spearheaded a campaign to grant women a designated place to sit in their workplaces. In 1924, she became one of the first women elected to the Madrid City Council, and in 1927 she was one of only thirteen women represented in the National Assembly of the Primo de Rivera dictatorship.

33. Nicolás Estévanez Murphy was a military officer and republican politician. He participated in the successful Revolution of 1868 but was imprisoned

The opinions of Catholics against divorce rest on the Gospels, in which, they believe, there is a law handed down from Jesus Christ himself on marriage and monogamy,[34] the basis of Church doctrine. This is false.

Catholic Church doctrine on marriage is incomplete, rough, and immoral. It is said to be taken from the Gospels; the Gospels speak of marriage very little, of divorce not at all; what they do talk about is polygamous marriage and the repudiation of marriage by the husband:[35] texts sing.

In Matthew 19 there is a reference to the Pharisees asking Jesus if it was lawful for a *man* to repudiate his marriage to his wife. Jesus answered that God had created the human race, male and female, which, yoked together, would be united as one flesh, and what was made by God cannot be unmade by man.

The Pharisees object to him that Moses permitted repudiation; Jesus answers that he did it because of the

---

a year later for joining the republican insurrection. Later he became minister of war during the first Spanish Republic. Among other things, he espoused anarchism, anticlericalism, atheism, and republicanism.

34. *Translator's note.* The Spanish term *monogamia* here refers to the practice of being with one person and no one else for the duration of one's life. This meaning of the English term *monogamy* is considered archaic; see "Monogamy, N. (2)," *Merriam-Webster*, 2023, www.merriam-webster.com/dictionary/monogamy.

35. *Translator's note. Repudiar* refers to when a man rejects his wife through legal channels, so that the marriage is broken off. Unlike *divorciar* ("divorce"), *repudiar* is something that, by definition, only a man can do.

hardness of the Jewish people's hearts, but in the beginning (?) it was not so. Therefore, "whoever repudiates *his wife*, except in cases where she has fornicated, is an adulterer if he takes another wife, and anyone who marries the repudiated woman is an adulterer." This same passage, described in almost the exact same way, is in chapter 10 of Mark, and . . . there is nothing else on earthly marriage in the Gospels.

In the rest of the New Testament there isn't much, either. Paul, in his First Epistle to the Corinthians (7.11–12), says, "The Lord commands, not I, that the wife must not separate from her husband, and if she separates, he commands that she remain unmarried or make peace with her husband. And the husband must not leave his wife."

If something can rightly be deduced from all this, it is the following (otherwise there is no common sense in the world or . . . in the New Testament): first, that for Jesus, the woman was property of the man, inescapably, once she was acquired. Second, while polygamy was permitted among those with whom Jesus was speaking, he does not condemn it or establish monogamy; what he does forbid is throwing women to the street and taking a woman thus thrown away. And third, he permits, not divorce, but repudiation of a woman for committing a carnal crime; for the man, we must stretch the text a little to include him under the same prohibition.

The loophole that *in the beginning*, an indeterminate time, there was no repudiation, is simply false: there was repudiation during the time of the patriarchs, and there is the story of Abraham to refute Jesus. The contrivances invented by theologians to reconcile these two contradictory things have only highlighted the contradiction more clearly.

Saint Paul later gives us an instruction on divorce: the woman may *separate* but not contract new bonds of marriage; that is it.

If the Church had wanted to preserve polygamy among Christians, it could find the basis for that in the Gospels, honorably interpreted. That did not suit the Church authorities, and they stood by the indissoluble bond of monogamy, but, finding fault with Jesus Christ, though without any such power to correct him, they restricted the permission he gives in the Gospel to repudiate the unfaithful spouse and built the doctrine in effect today on the foundation of absolute indissolubility.

But what a doctrine! For the Church, marriage is at once a sacrament and something like a necessary evil, a concession made reluctantly to human weakness that is, when compared to celibacy, a dirty, abject, contemptible status. The Church has placed before marriage twenty-four impediments! It has levied onerous taxes and required exasperating paperwork. It recognizes that marriage is a sacrament, that is, something excellent in its sanctity, but inferior to virginity, which is not a sacrament and which Christ did not say one word about. Moreover, it is incompatible with another sacrament, the holy orders,[36] although neither Paul, nor Jesus Christ, nor the apostles established this incompatibility.

The Church affirms that marriage is indissoluble, but in fact it does dissolve it, introducing for that purpose arbitrary distinctions that Jesus Christ and the apostles did not make and that thus are not recorded in the Holy Scripture. For example, if two spouses remain chaste during the first two months of their marriage, one of them, before the end of that term, may embrace a monastic life, even if that is repugnant to the other, but neither of them may separate in this very same way to marry another person or live free in the world.

Why? you ask the Church. Oh! it responds, this is a privilege for the sake of religion, but to get married or live an honest life among Christians—the Church doesn't consider that to be religious enough!

It allows that divorce, not repudiation, is in keeping with the Gospels, but with the condition that neither of the divorced spouses get remarried, and for this it imposes up to thousands of duros in duties and requires proceedings lasting no fewer than four years.[37] In fact, for the poor, divorce does not exist, and for the rich it is useless, since for each person to make an agreement to live their own lives, there is no need to spend money and endure four years of hassles, deposits, and other misfortunes.

---

36. The sacrament of holy orders (ordination) includes celibacy.
37. A duro was a coin equal to five pesetas.

And having established this brutal indissolubility, the Church nevertheless reserves the right to dissolve the marriages of rulers and magnates, so that the more powerful of the spouses may marry for *reasons of state*, but for the weaker spouse, it is off to a religious community.[38]

Don't ask the Church for anything else; it doesn't have it and can't conceive of it. Maybe if its ministers were married, it would be able to conceive of it, but they are celibate and, at the same time, polygamous men who accept and repudiate women when and how they please. For the people it is one doctrine and one set of rules of conduct; for the priests it is another set of rules and another secret doctrine; how delicious!

The Church has the entire social question and all possible other questions resolved, but say to the Church: an honorable man catches his wife in an act of adultery; understanding that she does not love him, he must separate from her—or a good woman's husband turns out to be a criminal who is condemned to life in prison. What should these poor people do? They must endure forced chastity, answers the priest as he thinks of his housekeeper or housekeepers.

---

38. *Translator's note. Príncipe* has been translated as "ruler" since it refers not to princes but to any head of state (as in Niccolo Machiavelli's *The Prince*). *Convento* has been translated as "religious community" because in Spanish (and sometimes in English) this word may refer to convents or monasteries, and there isn't anything else in the text to imply that the author was only talking about women being sent to a convent, even if that outcome was more likely.

"But this contradicts your doctrine," you say to him, "Marriage was instituted in order to soothe the natural concupiscence of the flesh, and so it is a good thing. These honorable people, being innocent, are deprived of this good thing that the Church gave to them by right, and not in vain, for their whole lives. That is why, apart from being contradictory to canon law, this precept is unjust and immoral."

Then the Church, cornered, confesses angrily that it doesn't have solutions for these cases or many others, and therefore its doctrine is imperfect and immoral.

Its final recourse is the following vulgarity: no one is innocent, at least from original sin (which was erased by baptism!); the hand of God is in all things, and so these innocents should resign themselves, because God has decided that they should be celibate and live helpless in their homes; this will suit them.

And beyond that, no one can get anything else out of the Church, because then it would have to confess that its doctrine does not come from Christ and that Christ did not teach any doctrine whatsoever on marriage and its contingencies; if the Church did that it would be suicide.

So, let anyone with common sense say whether this sociology will lead to anything and whether one can expect anything from someone who is supported by these doctrines and practices at this point, after the advances in the social sciences, anthropology, physiology, medicine, and the sum of all human knowledge of men.

My judgment—which I would not have expressed (since I believe no one would be interested in it) had you, Doña Carmen, not asked me, which is the same thing as ordering me—is favorable to divorce, prudently legislated, keeping in mind the children; above all, divorce is a necessary complement to the indignity of being married. The two examples above tell you everything there is to know about my thinking.

Those who have had the misfortune of an unbearable spouse will say if the clumsy theory of this man is Christian, if it is humane: "To those whose marriage is not going well, put up with it; it will be a lesson to others."

No, it will be a lesson against marriage and an incentive for free love because where is the brave man who can predict during his courtship that his spouse will be no good?

Injustice, an injustice as great as the sufferings of an innocent over the shortcomings of another, cannot be the law. But in order for total justice to triumph, there is an obstacle that must be removed wherever the Catholic, Apostolic, Roman Church exists; this must be the first divorce, that between the people and the Church.

JOSÉ FERRÁNDIZ[39]
Priest

---

39. José Ferrándiz y Ruiz was not only a priest but also a journalist, translator, and anticlerical writer.

The Spanish woman is not a proponent of divorce; when Ruiz Zorrilla introduced a new program of legislative reforms, one of his supporters was very surprised to see that it did not include divorce, and the head of the Republican Party answered, "We would have the women against us."

I believe the same thing, but I'm not sure if their opposition stems from being happy with their husbands or if they have such a low opinion of them that they are terrified of helping them satisfy their inconstant passions.

CONCEPCIÓN JIMENO DE FLAQUER[40]

Colombine—an incredibly meritorious writer—has had the courage to pose the exotic question of divorce in *Diario Universal*, calling on the most notorious names in the world of letters to participate in this plebiscite.

Outside their houses, all the intellectuals proclaim themselves to be in favor of divorce, but notice that for almost all of them, there is the tendency to develop their thesis from the point of view of adultery. And adultery can be *a motive*, but not *the* motive. Blasco Ibáñez and Sellés have already said this, the former protesting that marriage keeps two people who despise or hate each other

---

40. María de la Concepción Gimeno de Flaquer was a writer and an ideologically conservative feminist. At the time of this plebiscite, she had a good relationship with Burgos, but their relationship turned sour shortly thereafter. Note the misspelling of *Gimeno* in the text.

united as if on a single chain, and the latter, the illustrious author of *The Gordian Knot*,[41] asserting that the gossiping and manipulative woman, the free-spending woman who compromises the prestige and good name of her husband, and the short-tempered woman are worth no more than an adulteress.

Incompatibility of character is more than enough to dissolve a marriage. A woman can have one moment or a few moments of weakness but can still make her husband happy if she is discreet. An austere woman of rigid virtue can turn her home into a living hell, especially in a modest home where everything is common space and where there is no way to remove oneself or avoid each other.

An allegation of a moral violation is not necessary to break the bond of marriage. All that about morals is contingent on other things: between the Moor of Venice, who furiously strangles Desdemona, and the philosophical Philippine gobernadorcillo who lent his wife to the *castila*, there must be a prudent and convenient halfway point.[42]

But it occurs to me that for the greater Spanish society, divorce will end up being something like the coplas of Calaínos.[43]

---

41. Eugenio Sellés was a Spanish writer, playwright, journalist, and politician who studied law and had a successful career as a prosecutor. He was known as a journalist for his political essays.

42. A *gobernadorcillo* was a Philippine governor during the Spanish colonial period. *Castila* was what the local Filipinos called the Spaniards (who spoke Castilian).

43. Referring to words and reasoning that are not given any importance. Calaínos was a fictional knight-errant from the *Cancionero general* (*General*

Here, where there is no way out for a woman except through a cheap, hasty wedding and where a man goes to the church so blithely with his credential of six thousand reals or the two little stars on his sleeve, there is no need to think about divorce or anything else. God will provide!

Sir, did you do the budget for the house before getting married? No. Did you happen to flip through the civil code to find out what your rights and obligations were? No. So therefore you signed a blank contract with the same thoughtlessness as when signing a usurer's IOU when you want a handful of duros.

Is it worth it to discuss healing plans for catarrh with crazies who run into the street in shirtsleeves in the middle of winter at midnight?

It is said that there are also reasonable people who marry consciously, who find themselves disappointed by their bad luck. For their sake, it is necessary to establish divorce in Spain.

But divorce is the final step of our social sculpture, like a mosaic on the wall, whereas what we have now is a rough lower layer that hasn't even been sanded down yet. First it is necessary to instill in men the responsibility that comes with being head of the household, the money that is needed to maintain a home with decorum; in women it is necessary to root out the idea of extravagance in marriage, to make them understand it is better to earn two

---

Songbook), an anthology of lyric poetry from the late Middle Ages. *Coplas* refers to traditional verses.

pesetas than try to raise anemic children without good health or a future with one duro per day, such that they become witnesses to the *débâcle* of a home and the innocent victims of a stupid union.[44]

Divorce is not a bad topic to debate, but just go and try to discuss this with the eleven million Spaniards who cannot read or write.

And especially with women, who devote three hundred sixty-five days per year to searching out and capturing a husband, in the proportion of eleven women to one man, according to the latest statistics.

In Spain, divorce is a utopia. The brave ones who have already fallen for marriage know that there is no antidote for the pill they have swallowed.

If the wine is bad, don't drink it.

If the tobacco is terrible, don't smoke it.

If marriage is absurd, don't marry.

RICARDO GARCÍA DE VINUESA[45]
(From *La Democracia*)

---

44. *Translator's note. Matrimonio à outrance* is translated as "extravagance in marriage." The French term *à outrance* suggests going to extremes. The French was not kept, because in English *à outrance* means "to the bitter end," which might have incorrectly suggested a marriage to the bitter end (or monogamy). The French term *débâcle* means a "collapse" or a "breaking up."

45. Ricardo García de Vinuesa y Arguedas was a Civil Guard captain and translator.

Señora Colombine:

My very respected señora: I come with no titles other than my insignificance as a journalist to take part in this TRIAL OF DIVORCE, which you with such undeniable talent have brought before the Court of Public Opinion, a trial that has shown us, with its recognized jurisdiction, its zealous defenders from the Republic of Letters.

I don't know if I am qualified since I was not even a *witness* to the celebrated TRIAL OF MARRIAGE of Guerrero and Sepúlveda, but in my defense, I should state that at that time I was not yet in full possession of my civil rights, the result of my young age and especially my lack of qualifications.

If you with your better judgment deem this not to be sufficient grounds for a *challenge* to my *declaration* in your *trial*, below are a few ideas that may possibly be of some use.

As an enemy of establishing *negation*, and as my worthy coreligionist Señor Estévanez did a few days ago, deducing from it a concrete and categorical *affirmation*, I will employ the synthesis and brush aside the use of the syllogism.

Thus, I understand that the illustrious ex-minister of war dreams of an ideal of perfection in Humanity in better times, an ideal that surely many of us are chasing but that currently is very difficult to obtain, being that it is utopian due to the fact that it is inescapably impossible to overturn the ancient systems and the archaic foundational institutions that rule civilized societies.

There are those of us who, in order to promptly facilitate the resolution of the issue of the separation of Church and State, wish to seek the collective good by incorporating civil marriage into our traditions, since canon law has not been judged to be indispensable in the relationship between the individual and the State; but to go from this to denying the value, or more precisely, the necessity, of the legal personality of the marriage partnership leads to an abyss that can only traversed, after numerous centuries, by a perfectly organized and educated society.

Having been established now that civil marriage is an indispensable premise of social life and our relations, we should ask, is it necessary for legislators to agree to a measure that, while strengthening the above social institution, creates a sufficient guarantee that a spouse may, in the event that one of them may want to, at a given moment and for a certain reason, make free use of their will and effectuate another, new bond with a different person than the previous one, if that is their desire?

I am in favor of divorce, and therefore my response is in the affirmative, but with the caveat that divorce should not be conventional and casuistic, such as divorce that only allows for a separation of bodies, but rather that other, broader and more rational divorce on which I am writing here.

Provided that such a law is broad and flexible, the very frequent cases of bigamy and unmarried cohabitation, which unfortunately have now come to satisfy a need felt by all, would disappear.

Then no woman, whatever her status or condition may be, would, as is the case presently, have to resort to dissembling and guile, and what is even more painful, to drop off at an orphanage, in order to hide her shame, the fruit of her adultery and disgraceful relationships.

And do not object to me that a law to recognize paternity, such as the French Socialists have in their program, could remedy an offense of such magnitude, because such a law, once it is mulled over a bit, will be seen to be highly ridiculous and not at all practical.

The fact that divorce is an indispensable necessity to everyone is demonstrated by our fickle and inconstant human nature and is confirmed by the very nature of things.

To change position is the constant private yearning of any sick person, and all of us, absolutely all of us, have felt sick at one point or another because of a lack of freedom in our marriage.

This feeling, this yearning for freedom, innate in the spirit of man, is so spontaneous that no one believes they are free if they do not have free use of their conscience, their will, and their actions.

This is the reason why some thinkers have affirmed that the more one is free in one's actions, the more one is a slave.

A poet, Sully Prudhomme, wrote, "Caresses are nothing but anxious bliss, vain attempts of love to unite souls through a kiss."[46]

I believe that Goethe, in his *Elective Affinities*, sought out in vain, like Sully, a way to fuse together two souls in one. In the inorganic world the union of one or more molecules, or one or more atoms, is a self-evident truth, but in our world, in the world in which we live, the equilibrium is unstable.

Maupassant affirms, "I used to believe that a kiss from that woman would transport me to the heavens . . . and what a disappointment I suffered one day when, she being sick with some temporary fevers, I sensed on her breath a light, almost subtle whiff of human decay! Oh, the flesh!"

The flesh, yes, Señora Colombine, along with our gradual transformation, the thousand insubstantial whims, all the little nothings that constitute marriage, that sometimes make it monotonous, prosaic, and unbearable.

Ah, divorce! And then . . . then the unknown, which has not yet diminished our desires, the unexpected . . . That is what is lovely!

-----

46. *Translator's note.* The original French is "Les caresses ne sont que d'inquiets transports, / Infructueux essais du pauvre amour qui tente / L'impossible union des âmes par les corps"; Sully Prudhomme, *Euvres, Poésies, 1866–1872,* Alphonse Lemerre, p. 186. Prudhomme was the first winner of the Nobel Prize in Literature. Prieto's more literal translation into Spanish reads roughly as follows, in English: "Caresses are but anxious bliss, vain attempts of *poor love,* aspiring to the impossible union *of two souls* by means of their bodies" (emphasis added by Prieto in the Spanish text).

If one lives an ordinary, routine existence, as attached to one's customs as to one's childhood home . . . that's not my problem!

R. GARCÍA PRIETO[47]

Señora Colombine:

My dear and esteemed señora: To answer your kind letter, I would need to take some time in order to send you my reasoned opinion. However, I don't have an opinion and don't know when I will, and not wanting to delay my response any longer, I find myself begging your forgiveness. I am completely in favor of divorce, in the interests of morality and the dignity and sanctity of marriage, but since this is not about voting, but rather giving explanations, and also I don't know what opinions you have already collected, which I believe it would not be proper for me to disregard, it would be pointless to publish mine.

I hope that you will be so kind as to forgive me. Warmest regards,

FRANCISCO GINER

---

47. Manuel García Prieto was a Spanish lawyer and politician.

To Colombine:

Ay, my friend! You've come calling at the door of my little corner where I've been holed up for so long, surrendered to the weight of the years and my troubles. Forgotten by the world, I can't even remember the world of letters, which was always my pleasure. You've awakened me from my sleep to ask my opinion on *divorce*, a question that, like medals, has an obverse and a reverse, and I could not refuse someone whom I esteem so highly for her talent; but you forget that what you are asking of me I have addressed extensively in one of the various editions of *Trial of Marriage*, which I published, in verse, with my partner Ricardo Sepúlveda. There I convened distinguished writers, who honored the book with their well-known ingenuity.

When the debate began, I summoned them with a few quatrains, one of which I will copy below to present my opinion from that time in which I felt so fortunate with the holy companion of my own life, a life that I will soon be *divorcing,* as is the will of God, *who is the only one who can separate those whom He has joined together,* as Christ said in the Gospel of Matthew. Asked whether divorce was beneficial, I wrote,

> It's not for my sake I whine,
> but if a law came to force
> me and my wife to divorce
> I'd marry her twenty more times.

Vital Aza recorded in one of his brilliant quintets:

> I've meditated and thought on it,
> and see no good reason why a varlet
> should go and rupture his sacred bond.
> No señor! You may wish to abscond,
> but you'll just have to grin and bear it!

And the inspired poet Velarde said to me, starting with one of his famous tercets:

> Does the matter of divorce make you feel dreary?
> Come to my home, and you will see your weary soul
> come straight to life and turn you quite cheery.

The French writer M. Ricard[48] tells how a crazy man caged a sparrowhawk with a dove, and then left. Later he returned with a wise man who, seeing that the sparrowhawk was furious and the dove was covered with blood, freed them, and the very happy birds flew away. What we have here is wisdom putting *divorce* into practice, the only way to punish the husband for his tyranny and the wife for her weakness.

But the children! It is true that they are the victims of marital discord, but since it does not teach them anything good and causes them to stop loving their family, it

---

48. Louis-Xavier de Ricard, a French poet and journalist who founded the short-lived, progressive, and controversial literary and scientific magazine *La revue.*

is considered beneficial to separate them from a disturbed home.

But what am I saying, what am I once again writing? Some may think that I am writing this for myself, but all I'm actually doing is scrutinizing the fields of another.

My friend, Colombine, look in the abovementioned *Trial*, at what Leopoldo Cano, José Herrero, Joaquina Balmaseda, Constantino Gil, Fernández Shaw, Suárez Bravo, Manuel Valcárcel, Tolosa Latour, Enrique R. Solís, Father Fita, and the marchioness of Valmar, among other first-rate authors, opined with courageous words, superb verses, or excellent prose. And these opinions still don't give any results in Spain, despite the fact that divorce is accepted in almost every country. Montesquieu already said, "Divorce is necessary in advanced civilizations."

The philosopher Erasmus teaches us that "it was necessary to respect marriage while it was no more than a purgatory and to dissolve it when it came to be a hell."

The famous Champfort writes, "Divorce is so natural that in many houses it lies down every night between the husband and wife."

Don't ask me today if I will sing the palinode, because I will answer, "How times change! Am I by chance the same, alone, except without the happiness I had in my loving home?"

Victor Hugo writes, "Love is to be two and to be but one; two beings merged in one angel is heaven." And the satirical Englishman Lord Byron, to support the idea, allowed himself to write, "Marriage from love, like vinegar from wine." How much I battled this thought!

It was in my *Salon Stories* and all my propagandistic books on the holy bond. Yes, because two people who go to the altar truly in love are like two drops of water that mix and commingle such that nobody can separate them. For them *divorce* is impossible.

In contrast, those who are dragged to the church by greed or calculation leave their hearts at the door; they are like two drops, one water and the other oil; they join, but they don't mix and commingle. *Divorce* imposes itself. The poor children they make!

If my partner Sepúlveda were to read these sloppy lines, which neither assert nor reject anything, he would open his eyes as wide as can be, as it would be hard for him to believe these lines were written by the same hand as wrote our *Trial*. Does he think the same way, then? Hadn't he had it with marriage, and didn't he get married twice? And he is very happy today! He has the floor now to give his opinion in this new trial conducted by *Diario Universal*.

What one writes while sleeping, one erases upon awakening. Rip up these quatrains and allow me to sleep until God grants me my eternal rest, which won't be long.

TEODORO GUERRERO[49]

---

49. Born in Cuba, Teodoro Guerrero Pallarés was a writer, journalist, and politician of the Liberal-Conservative Party who was educated in Spain and lived in Havana and Madrid, where he died in 1904.

Friend Colombine:

My opinion on divorce? It is very simple and pleasing to everyone. Divorce is disunion—the opposite of marriage, which is union: *conjuntio maris et fœminæ*, as Modestinus defined it.[50]

Now, this union of souls, wills, and bodily realities has two aspects: legal and religious; one is the purview of the law, independent of any confession; the other is the purview of the conscience of the believer.

The law is either natural or civil. Perpetual unions cannot be imposed on nature; with respect to civil law, there is no reason to authorize such unions. Nature only recognizes desire, the law a contract—both are temporary and ephemeral.

Religion gives unions a different character—it either loosens or tightens the bond, extends or restricts it according to one's creed. So the Christian believes the bond to be indissoluble and advocates monogamy, and the Muslim allows polygamy and repudiation.

In dubiis libertas:[51] among so many affirmations encountered, liberty for each to follow their faith or the dictates of their mind.

---

50. Latin for "the conjunction of man and woman."
51. The full Latin saying is *In necessariis unitas, in dubiis libertas, in omnibus caritas*, meaning "In necessary things unity, in uncertain things liberty, in all things charity."

Natural law leaves us to the mercy of our own impulses; civil law should simply regulate contracts, which can be dissolved.

And whoever is Catholic should obey the Council of Trent and maintain the indissolubility of the link, and anyone who rejects this and wishes to become a Muslim should be free to have his appropriate harem.

What is not possible is to be Catholic and maintain divorce *quod ad vinculum*.[52] That would be like making a hare pie without the hare.

There is a place for divorce inside the Church: the one applied by a certain crafty priest to a couple he had married, who came to him to undo their bond the following month.

"Kneel, my children," he said, and taking the aspergillum, *pim*, *pam*, he started beating them over the head with it one by one.

"Father, what is this?" said the two of them, seeing themselves beaten this way. And the good priest, without flinching, continued landing his equal blows with the aspergillum, harder and harder.

"But what is this?" exclaimed the two, alarmed now and with bumps all over their heads.

"It's nothing, my children," said the priest. "The way to undo the marriage is for you to endure this until only one of you is left to tell the story."

---

52. The Council of Trent was established to declare Protestantism heresy. Among other things, it distinguished between *divortium quo ad thorum* ("legal separation") and *divortium quo ad vinculum* ("divorce").

One must Christianly suffer the blows of adversity until . . . this. There, now you know my opinion.

ANTONIO LEDESMA[53]

To Colombine:

My charming friend: You have put me in a bind by asking me my opinion on divorce. If we are to be logical, then a husband who is so perfectly suited to his wife, as I am, must unavoidably show himself to be an adversary of anything that could undo the bond of marriage.

But if we reason it out slowly, thinking about those who do not live as I do, maybe we would conclude that divorce, in certain cases, is the only way to prevent two people from being unhappy.

In my judgment, dear friend, it would be best if those who believed in the necessity of divorce did not ever get married.

ÁNGEL DE LUQUE[54]

---

53. Antonio Ledesma Hernández was a lawyer, writer, and proponent of regenerationism, a school of thought influenced by Krausism and opposed to the corrupt political system of Spain that institutionalized the deliberate alternation of governing powers between the Liberal and Conservative Parties, often done with bribery and fraud to ensure the desired results.

54. Ángel de Luque was an intellectual and translator of foreign literature into Spanish, including Émile Zola's *Germinal* and several short stories by Wilkie Collins.

Señora Colombine:

Quod Deus conjunxit homo non separet.[55]

An illustrious writer once said that the best thing that
could be said about the Christian religion is that it has sub-
sisted despite the harm done to it by those who profess it.
Well, that is what I say about marriage. After all, can there
by anything better to see, in these times of doubt, than the
spectacle of a young and happy couple that leaves the
church united to begin a life of love and mutual sacrifice?
Or the old couple who support each other as they walk
down the street, having finished their life's mission, the
little old man awaiting death next to his little old wife?
Surely a more beautiful and consoling image does not exist, but unfortunately, I know so few happily married
couples, yet I know of so many unhappy ones that I have
come to wonder whether it would be good to change the
laws on this point. To find a foot to stand on, I have thoroughly read and analyzed, along with other very recom-
mended works, a book by Díez Enríquez titled *Positive
Rights of Women*, and reading this wonderful and useful
book has confirmed to me the idea that it is necessary to
amend the code with respect to women, not only in this
specific case, but also in many others.

Although I am no *feminista enragé*, I truly understand
that the law is extremely unjust. As the same notable

---

55. "What God has joined together, let no man separate."

jurisconsult says, "One's sex may alter one's tastes and inclinations, but it does not change a person's qualities. Consequently, neither does the law. The two sexes should be equal before the fundamental and derived laws, before the legal system. But the current limited rights of women have as their origin women's traditional lack of cultivation, their glorified frivolity. And before the force of this overwhelming belief, before the imperium of age-old customs, we can only trust but in the small victories that reason gradually gains over the prevailing preoccupations."

But confining ourselves to the original matter, I should state that, indeed, the inequality between men and women established in the civil code is not, nor can it ever be, justified in any way, as article 56 makes no distinction whatsoever between the sexes. It says, "The spouses are obliged to live together, be faithful, and mutually help one another." In contrast, in articles 438 (paragraphs 1, 2, and 4) and 452, there is a radical difference, to the point of allowing the unfaithful wife to be killed while applying an insignificant punishment to the husband who has broken his oath. Also, the way divorce is permitted here, the husband always has dominion over his wife, such that when the spouses separate civilly and canonically, the husband, taking advantage of the complete liberty that is de facto granted him by the current law and social depravity, may lead whatever life suits him best; meanwhile, the wife, always a slave to conventions, may not, without damaging her own dignity, love another man; but if the husband chooses to leave his wife and thus forget his sense of decency, he has the right to *shut her away inside her home, punish her, and even kill her,* risking no more than exile for *six months to six years* in the latter case.

Is this fair? Can such a disturbing difference be tolerated? Without a doubt, no. We should try to win divorce here as it has been established in France, so that when the couple separates, each person can live in freedom to contract a new bond. What then? The woman who was in love when she married, believing as a result of her affection that her husband possessed all the best qualities imaginable, and who later finds herself *united forever* to a brutal, despotic, unfaithful, or squandering person—is it fair for her to endure such martyrdom, *dragging a heavy chain for all eternity,* even if she has separated from him? Of course not. And for the record, I feel the same way in the opposite case.

I believe then, that the Church and State, by agreement, should establish *absolute divorce* as the only way to avoid innumerable irregular unions and unhappy marriages.

Some may say that the remedy is extreme, maybe very dangerous, but to this I would answer that only those who are sick, and who need to, will make use of it. Certainly, good and loving husbands whose affection is requited by their wives will not ask for this, nor will those men who have married for convenience and who find themselves having to patiently endure the burden that they have created for themselves; nor will the women who have resigned themselves to suffer the frustrations caused by their husbands, who love them despite everything. None of these people will ask for divorce, but there will be so many others for whom divorce will be salvation!

As for me, I declare that this matter does not touch me personally, not up close and not from a distance, and I am only speaking from a perspective of general interest, basing my arguments on what I have heard and read from many men of talent, including my good friends Zozaya and Gómez Carrillo, as well as the many apt things that Diez Enríquez says in his book, supported by my illustrious colleagues from the *Revista de los Tribunales*, but mainly and above all, I base my arguments on the sad real-life examples we see every day that have caused many people to look upon marriage with the same terror with which they would see an abyss at their feet whose depth they cannot fathom. All that about *Quod Deus conjunxit homo non separet* is very beautiful, but when that phrase was written the people used torches for illumination, while today electricity gives light everywhere. The people were better back then, or at least they appeared so. They had not yet discovered *neurosis* or such things that were just as, or even more, important. It was not so ridiculous to truly fall in love, nor to be a slave to a pledged word, and death was preferable to dishonor. Today the opposite is true, and consequently we must modernize our laws. To new years new customs.[56]

EVA MARTÍNEZ DAZA[57]

---

56. This last sentence was written in English and italicized in the source text.

57. Eva Martínez Daza was an Andalusian writer and journalist.

Señora Colombine:

My dear esteemed señora: Given my occupations in the position I exercise and the daily parliamentary work in which I find myself immersed, I do not have the pleasure of satisfying your request, due to an absolute lack of time, but not desire. I defer to you who have written to me so kindly in your letter from the twenty-fifth.

Warmest regards,

ANTONIO MAURA[58]

Divorce

Colombine, of *Diario Universal*, has asked my opinion on divorce: will the distinguished writer allow me to expound my views from the pages of this new platform?

I am in favor of divorce: I am divorced. I am divorced not once, not twice, not thrice but four times.

And I will tell you all how I did this stupendous thing. When I oftentimes think of those serious problems that plague many of us but, fortunately, not me, I usually ask myself, "What would I do if faced with this formidable obstacle? What would be my attitude if capricious circumstances had taken me down *that* road, rather than this very different road I am now on?"

---

58. See note 14.

And then for a minute, my imagination wanders along that other road, and during this moment I think of myself as if I were *someone else*. And so I have been married; I have adored various women whom I was sincerely fond of, with whom I would have gladly entered into holy union (and this was what I sometimes told them). And what good fortune and adversities have I had in married life?

I see myself walking up a narrow, dark hallway leading to a fifth-floor apartment. I'm inside a small, shabby room with no rugs, no paintings, no curtains, no furniture, no fireplace.

I see myself wearing a suit I bought from El Águila for fifty pesetas, or maybe another suit I bought that hasn't been tailored, and every day because of it I am forced to say I am not home, when I am.

I see myself at all hours sitting at a news desk, attached to the terrible yoke of a newspaper, blathering out political articles or literary narrative pieces, feeling an enthusiasm I don't feel, faking a hate that doesn't pass through my spirit. And then, when I have returned home, I see myself taking the pen again and writing bland, flavorless translations, or short stories and articles that I take to the magazines and newspapers, in my frayed suit, which they accept grumblingly, out of pity.

I see myself standing next to my wife (on one of those rare, unavoidable occasions when we poor literati, who are ashamed of our wives, find ourselves obliged to go out on a walk with them); I see myself with her, and she is wearing one of those indeterminate old dresses she has made new with her feminine skill, which inspire more compassion than a dress that is obviously old or obviously worn out. I see myself at home on one of those terrible, all-too-frequent days when there is no more credit and no more money, exasperated, brutal, violent, screeching while my wife is screeching, blaspheming as my children are crying, forced to move to another fifth-floor apartment, from which we will move again in a month's time, forced once again to go, humiliated, ashamed, to the newspaper or magazine that took my article last week, and they don't want another one . . .

And when I get here, I set my quill down on the table and put my head in my hands, thinking. And you wouldn't think it possible to imagine, with an imagination like Dante's, two different hells, equally horrid, but I do see another one. I'm on the outskirts of a town in La Mancha, and it is gray, monotonous, desolate, no water no trees.

A road snakes in the blackish plain, through the enormous squares of farm plots, through plantations of gray olive trees, and every evening along this street (after my meal in wintertime or at nightfall in the summer) a señor comes, and he is neither young nor old, and he doesn't have the vivacity of youth or the indolence of old age, but his appearance and his gestures reveal a deep exhaustion. And if you come close to him and listen to his words, you will realize that this man who was once intelligent, alive, generous, *bold, enterprising* is now an unhappy automaton. This man used to be an ingenious and cultured writer: he read the classics and contemporary works; he wrote free and ingenious words; he enjoyed a certain reputation that encouraged him in his work. And now he lives holed up and silent in this town. He gets up at the same hour every day; all the minutes of his life are the same; the bells of the town's eight or ten churches toll constantly; his wife has filled the house with saints and lit candles; the devout who enter the house in mourning with their rosaries talk to her of their sadness and of death; the sharecroppers don't pay their rent because they've lost their harvest; the poor tenants also cannot pay their rent; they need to buy a new team of oxen to replace the old one, but there is no money; they urgently need to make a repair in a building, and they are forced to take out a loan with interest . . .

And later, on top of all these obsessions of his spirit, the details of his daily private life make him feel desperate—a calm yet fierce desperation that is no longer expressed as screams, or insults, or curses, or punches. The bedrooms are dirty, messy; if someone attempts to clean them, they make a racket as they drag the furniture around and mix everything up; books and papers disappear from the table of his office, and he can't find them when he needs them; on the dining room table are some diapers and a comb; when he wakes up in the morning, there's no water in the jug; meals are never ready on time; if by chance he sits down to do some work for a while, remembering his old loves from his literary artist days, they start cleaning the room next door, or his wife comes into the office with her sewing machine—because as I said, they're cleaning the room next door—and she'll be sewing there all afternoon, while he abandons his plans, resigned . . .

And then on top of all this, all the economic anguish and the constant, intolerable annoyances in their private lives, there is the moral and intellectual isolation in which he finds himself. Who is there to talk to? Who is there to discuss his spirit's dreams and memories? His name has now been forgotten in Madrid: his old buddies don't remember him. But from time to time he feels a yearning, a desire, a longing for his productive life of freedom . . . And then he leaves his house, leaves behind his dark town, and takes a walk by himself along the tortuous road in the vast gray plain planted with gray olive trees.

And when I get here, I once again put my quill down on the table and put my head in my hands, thinking. These two women have been my women; my destiny has been tied to their destinies. Now I am free in my bachelor apartment, sitting at my table with my papers, my pens, and my books, happy with my cape and my bohemian hat, writing whatever I want, jumping from one newspaper to the next, not held back worrying about "the children's bread," not having to be humiliated because of the rent, doing nothing when it pleases me to do nothing.

Señora, this is how I have been divorced without being divorced.

J. MARTÍNEZ RUIZ[59]
(From *España*)

---

59. Later this year, 1904, the novelist, playwright, and literary critic José Augusto Trinidad Martínez Ruiz began using the pseudonym Azorín, from a character in one of his books. Martínez Ruiz was a radical in the 1890s but began moving to the right by 1899. He served as a Conservative deputy between 1907 and 1919.

Excerpt

Something analogous can be said about the character of Mauricio, a noble and lofty spirit, a fine and trusting soul, whose concept of love is high enough to know that when the specter of an intruder must always rear its head between two souls, reconciliation between them is impossible.* And Mauricio's concept of life is broad enough for him to know that existence is not simply defined by a woman's faithfulness and that love, no matter how grand and pure it may be, does not necessarily have to last forever. When his marriage is broken off, he does not believe his life is over, and he is even able to end the drama with a note of hope:

"You will be happy," he says to his wife, and then he adds, "and who knows, maybe I will be too." How far this is from the famous *tue-la*[60] that is so pleasing to our matador playwrights, who only know how to end their plays like a running of the bulls, with a couple of characters dragged away!

No one can accuse the ending of Capus's play of being outside the realm of what is human. It reveals an evolution of spirits, and over in France, where so many plays have been written in so many ways against the divorce

* From the review of the play *El adversario*. [*L'adversaire* (*The Adversary*), by Alfred Capus and Emmanuel Arène (1903)]

---

60. French for "kill her."

law, it is another argument in favor of it, without the tedious rhetoric or emphatic speeches that were so fashionable on both sides of the Pyrenees a few years back. A woman is unfaithful to her husband, and the husband believes it impossible to remake their life of peace and love. The problem is easily resolved through divorce. Is someone going to say this is absurd because there is no spilling of blood, and instead of a revolver to cut the Gordian knot, a law bursts onto the scene like a deus ex machina?

ALEJANDRO MIQUIS[61]

Señora Colombine:

My dear señora: I am very sorry for not being able to answer your question. I am single and have no opinion on marriage, let alone divorce.

Very sincerely,

F. NAVARRO Y LEDESMA[62]

Señora Colombine:

I believe that the ability to rescind a contract with grounds is the best guarantee of its success. In the legal

---

61. Pen name of the drama critic Anselmo González.
62. Francisco Navarro y Ledesma was a journalist and literary critic.

order and in the moral order, divorce is reasonable. That is why I doubt we will accept it any time soon. It will take a bit of work.

A good rule of prudence is to thoroughly study before entering any unknown place, but prudence will be left behind if you do not also, and preferably, study your exit.

This is my opinion, and I am sure we are in the majority . . . theoretically. In practice, to see reason, we will need to be beaten over the head with this idea.

Otherwise, it will take time.

Your devoted friend and admirer,

JOSÉ NOGALES[63]

Señora Colombine:

Dear esteemed señora: Family issues and illnesses at home have prevented me from keeping my promise to you and writing something on *divorce*. Might you be aware that twenty years ago, I staged a drama in the Español [Theater], titled *The Heart of Man*, the subject of which was the defense of divorce. At the same time in the Comedia, I was rehearsing another one called *A Man of Heart*, attacking and ridiculing divorce. This second one never made it to the stage because I thought it was bad. I withdrew it and tore it up.

---

63. José Nogales Nogales was a journalist and writer who is sometimes included in the Generation of '98.

You can deduce the implications yourself.

My very personal opinion is that I would remarry a hundred times over the woman who is my wife, thanks to God, but I would excuse many unfortunates who throw their wives off the balcony.

Your admirer,

PEDRO DE NOVO Y COLSON[64]

Señora Colombine:

Humbly, and I consider humility to be a virtue and something inspiring, I will tell you my opinion on divorce. I am in favor of it, and in declaring this, I also declare, while we're at it, that I'm in favor of marriage, the opposite of our young supermen who believe they see in marriage a dagger for Art.

I've made my confession: in favor of marriage, first, and in favor of divorce, later—oh yes, this is funny—so that the mistake can be unmade.

Since love does not bind us with iron but with roses, and roses are—fortunately, and despite the disparagers of poetry—beautifully fragile, the ties of love can be broken. If they are broken, that is sad—it is always sad when one does not live in kindness—but they can be quite broken because—and this image is a good one—to go out for

---

64. Pedro de Novo y Colson was a historian, poet, playwright, sailor, and member of the Royal Spanish Academy and the Royal Academy of History.

a walk with an enemy is not an understandable pleasure; it is better to go by yourself . . . I believe that—no matter how ordinary the lives of so many are—all of us, in this poor and rich world, "have something to do." I believe this. And often this "something" can be smothered in the hands of the forced continuation of marriage.

I love liberty—*"Who doesn't love the day?"* Núñez de Arce said, and divorce is sometimes a dithyramb[65] to liberty. If two hearts hate each other or cordially repudiate each other, they do well to separate; each one, alone, may spend their days better than in a mistaken collaboration. In this act, I see sincerity—sincere hate has a nobility. And isn't it an unpleasant hypocrisy when two people who hate each other, or don't love each other well, live together? No, no. No hypocrisy. It is better for the heart to say its truths, and thus the social facts will clearly win.

Let's love each other today. If we abhor each other tomorrow, let's separate. But let's love each other well, so that we won't have to separate; that is better . . .

Your humble friend and reader,

J. ORTIZ DE PINEDO[66]

---

65. Among other things, a dithyramb is an ancient Greek hymn, especially one in praise to Dionysus. The Spanish word *ditirambo* also means exaggerated or excessive praise.

66. José Ortiz de Pinedo wrote poetry, prose, and drama with a leftist bent.

Señora Colombine:

My friend, your order arrived (because we caballeros consider a request from a judicious woman to be an order) right as I was finishing an excellent book by the academic Señor Beltrán y Rózpide titled *The Hispano-American Peoples of the Twentieth Century*, a work that still perfumes my office with the suggestive scent of the printing press when the white pages are fresh off the machine, adorned with the flowers of thought.

My senses are in all things American now, so my head, already weak to begin with, has been enmeshed in concerns from *across the seas*, as any old haggard academic would say, and I can barely fathom anything that has to do with anything else.

But, what I have here is that—and mathematics is useful in everything, as the apothecary from the story says—in studying all things pertaining to the *continente colombino*,[67] suddenly the issue of divorce jumps before my eyes.

Sr. Beltrán analyzes something referring to the Argentine Republic and says, "Among domestic affairs regarding the political and social life of the Republic, the ones that have been, and still are, the most interesting over these past few years, that is, the first few years of this century, are the draft legislation on divorce, the electoral fraud, and the upcoming renewal of the presidency.

---

67. *"Continente colombino"* refers to the Americas.

"Deputy Olivera put forth the divorce bill. Argentine ladies have had several meetings to protest the proposed reform and find themselves very resolute in their decision to make use of all legal means to defend the indissolubility of the marriage bond. In contrast, there were public conferences in favor of divorce at the Women's Socialist Club; women filled the hall, applauded, and endured speeches such as the one by an Italian orator who spoke from eight in the evening until twelve midnight.

"Their mood very impassioned, the public practically stormed the Congress, keen to hear anything that was said in favor of and against the indissolubility of marriage. Opinion was very divided in the Chamber, and the result was uncertain; friends and adversaries of divorce made extreme efforts to obtain their triumph; good speeches were made, and when it came time to vote, the bill was rejected by only two votes (50 to 48)."

To advance my opinion, I will say that if I had been a deputy in Argentina, I would have voted with the majority on the above bill, but actually, things there are not like in Spain; there, public opinion, composed of émigrés from all over the world, formed by people with extremely radical and socially modernist ideas, a public opinion that goes by automobile and produces vertigo—I repeat— there, public opinion sways and turns even the most prudent individuals upside down.

In our country, the issue of divorce will not come up for centuries and should not weigh on us because maybe when the solution is close at hand, they will have repented what they have done in other places; meanwhile, we will have progressed in perfecting the family and improving the home and society in general, and we will be prepared to withstand these dangerous tests.

Many, extremely many tons of paper have been used on the advantages and disadvantages of divorce, and I believe we are in the same place today as we were before.

The injustices committed against women, the inequality between the sexes, the torture of a life filled with evils and pain, the misfortunes of the children, the profaned home, the compromised virtue, the triumph of power and money; all of this and more comes out in books and newspapers, in dramas and comedies, and in speeches and perorations.

And yet, have we come to a better understanding? Have there been any decisive leanings on the part of society in general? Frankly, I would say we have made no progress whatsoever. Naquet, the author of the legislation that was so hotly contested in the French Chamber, Naquet, a learned man, a man of energy and conviction, has felt himself vacillate, has meditated, and finally has regretted his actions.

So, what will they do, those who have taken on this issue because they wanted a bit of swordplay of the imagination and a hobby at the public protest?

A marriage gone bad is hell, certainly, if God does not answer one's prayers—the prayers of the woman almost always, and sometimes the supplications of the man.

I remember well what I read in the *Life of Saint Monica*, by Monseigneur Bougaud: "Nothing sadder than the first season of a difficult union; a dream vanishes every day, and the fantasies disappear one by one like the leaves of trees on autumn days. The partners discover inequality and the opposition of their characters, the differences in how they see things, and finally the harshest reality comes; and if faith, love, and reflection were not to help us, we would drop in prostration, we would be seized by discouragement, and hope would disappear forever."

The portrait is as sad as it is apt; but the coin has its reverse side; and pictured on this reverse side in this case is the divine figure of the mother of Saint Augustine, who, despite the weariness and the detachment caused to her husband Patricio by her prayers, works of charity, and sweetness, always preserved a peace in her soul, guided her son to goodness and glory, and came to love the man who looked down at her; and, filling her life with hopes and yearning for the greater good, she lived on the earth smiling and calm.

We must agree that the most perfect thing up to now in rules of marriage, separation, and divorce has been Christianity and the canonic law born from it: *The man will leave his father and mother and unite with his wife, and they will be two of one flesh. No man may separate what God has joined together.*

God always at the front!

If we want marriage to lose that which everyone attributes to it, inspiration, and become a simple agreement, a trade, like a pair of animals, well then—oh, well then!—there's nothing to discuss; we'll just stick to the contract.

I believe that the Christian religion clearly set out the issue we are discussing. Do we want Christ not to intervene? Chaos, then.

If we abandon religion, do without it, we don't know where to turn to regulate married life; we might as well say it would be best to live without any obstacles or rules of behavior; let the years go by; let us approach the fatal end of our lives with no guide for the present, nothing to light the future, and, closing our eyes, let us throw ourselves into the stormy sea, with no shore in sight, into the bottomless abyss.

The next observation is so indisputable I don't remember who the first person was that made it! The more the man and wife maintain a living connection between them as they look into each other's eyes, the more they repress, he his habits of male autonomy, and she the enchantments of her feminine wiles, the stronger their mutual affection will be, the greater will be the delights of marriage—stronger and gentler at the same time, the sweet ties that bind them; and love will grow, will every day become more and more dignified and noble, without their ever feeling the desire for divorce.

Love and duty, closely united, is the solution to this matter that preoccupies us so much.

Duty, the divine brother of work, as Legouvé says repeatedly; duty, the God of strong souls, savior of the weak, permanent counselor, consolation at all hours, the one steady thing in this world of constant change—one cannot invoke your name without bowing one's head . . . duty, duty, you are one of the greatest and most eternal counterweights of humanity; you are contrary to divorce.

For duty, wealth is an obligation to sacrifice; poverty, to consoling teachings; power, to a burden; liberty, to restraint; love, to true love—infinite life in everlasting contact with God, which does not brook radical separations, does not brook divorces that break the harmony of creation.

If absolute divorce existed everywhere on earth, and if the law did not lock it away in a strong, very tight circle, the world would be the tremendous antechamber of the most horrific and unimaginable hell.

JESÚS PANDO Y VALLE[68]

Señora Colombine:

Dear esteemed señora: I did not answer you because I have no opinion whatsoever on divorce, and as such it is not possible for me to tell you what that opinion is. I would need to spend some time studying this matter, and I don't have any time. Since my silence might seem impo-

---

68. Jesús Pando y Valle was an Asturian journalist, poet, and writer who held positions in various government ministries.

lite, I am responding to you anyway and am using this occasion to send you my greetings.

Sincerely,

EMILIA PARDO BAZÁN[69]

The love of those who love each other perfectly does not increase because they get married, or decrease because they don't, and those who do not love each other do not need divorce to separate.

Those who have not found happiness in marriage have the right to procure it elsewhere, and it is better that they search for it under the shadow of the law than in the shadow of crime.

Neither religions nor codes could ever stop someone who, when married, was cheated on, or cheated, from searching for a new love or the fantasy of it.

The children of those who divorce cannot be more unhappy than the children of those who cheat, and it is preferable to have parents who confess their mistake than parents who have betrayed one another.

---

69. Emilia Pardo Bazán y de la Rúa-Figueroa was born into an affluent family in Galicia and was a countess. She became a renowned novelist, literary critic, playwright, and professor and was an important early feminist and champion of women's rights. In 1906, she became the first woman to head the literature section of the Madrid Atheneum. She is best known for her novel *Los pazos de Ulloa* (*The House of Ulloa*; 1886) and short stories such as "Las medias rojas" ("The Red Stockings"; 1887).

Divorce is more favorable to the woman than to the man, because the disadvantages of marriage are greater for her.

As long as marriage remains too expensive for many to afford, adultery will be the freeloader scrounging at the table of love.

JACINTO OCTAVIO PICÓN[70]

Friend Colombine:

My many occupations are partly to blame for not having answered your letter of petition, and also partly to blame is the exact nature of the question you have formulated. On extremely rare occasions have I thought about this trial of divorce, but when I did, so many varied reflections surfaced in my mind that I preferred to set it aside, understanding that nothing was drawing me into these discourses. Religion, evolutionist morality, human physiology, pathology, and life experience, among other things, quickly arose as informants to my reflections, and seeing that each one brought its own contingent of facts and logic, I said to myself, Is someone ordering me to get involved in this business?

Nevertheless, as with anything involving human destiny, I hold the fundamental idea that one of the strongest,

---

70. Jacinto Octavio Picón Bouchet was a writer, painter, art critic, and journalist who wrote in the style of costumbrismo.

most invariable, and most beneficial intentions of progress is for humanity to continue to root out the cursed bane of our miserable lives, the idea that "Redemption is not possible," "There is no remedy," which should only be used to talk of death, and since I believe that there should be a sedative for every intense pain, hope for all despair, clemency for all sentences, a correction for every mistake, and a coming together in any affinity, I accept divorce, since it can often be medicine, rebirth, a modification, and a redemption that can prevent crime, insanity, or the total annulment of a human being.

Humanity will continue to eliminate its awful bonds to see if it can reduce its grave suffering. Whether sooner or later, divorce will become one of a number of indisputable remedies of social therapy, used by those in need of it.

Sincerely,

ÁNGEL PULIDO[71]

Señora Colombine:

My good friend: Divorce is nothing but stalling and a palliative. The only—the great—remedy would be to destroy the current family, destroy the way it is organized,

---

71. Ángel Pulido Fernández was a doctor and politician. In 1904 he took up the cause of Filosefardismo, a movement seeking to establish the rights of Sephardic Jews, whose ancestors were expelled from Spain during the Inquisition.

and scrape the idea of it out of our minds. Master and lord is the father; a slave, his woman; property of the two, the children, whom we make Protestant or Catholic, inculcate with our own defects, and give wonderful thrashings to to put them on the path of virtue.

So, I have not seriously meditated on divorce; I haven't formed a judgment on divorce and couldn't send you two more lines about it without revealing the vacuity and superficiality of my reasoning, but, friend Colombine, I have a terrible book on divorce, and I am sending it to you as a gift.

This book, published in London in 1769, was banned by the Inquisition, with first-class censorship, and I've seen it in the *Index Expurgatorius*,[72] marked with the tragic little hand, which seems to say to us with its forefinger angrily extended, *"This is an abomination!"* This book, banned even for those who were authorized to read prohibited books, opens with the "cry of an honorable man who believes he is authorized by divine and natural right to repudiate his wife." I have read this cry and can assure you, friend Colombine, that it is a terrible thing to see a man in this kind of screaming trance.

Later this book has a *Legislation on Divorce*, the preamble of which says many sensible and substantial things, and ends with *Divorce Demanded by the Countess of X****.

All of it anonymous, all of it written in the mid-eighteenth century, during a time of debased morals in a

---

72. A catalog of books prohibited by the Catholic Church.

Europe before the French Revolution. I needn't say more for you to intensely see how this book is a book of pain, desperation, and enormous and infinite grief. Also, this book is a bibliographic gem. It is not in the National Library; I have not seen it in any bookstore catalog. But don't think that I am trying to talk up the value of this gift; this cost me no more than one real in a stand in El Rastro. What I would like is for you to commit to translating this book and publishing it for us.

It is a terrible book. I swear to you if I had read it before getting married, I would not have gotten married. Fortunately, the cry of this man, and the whining and sniffling of this mysterious countess came to my ears after several years of her being tied to the respectable and venerated rope of a husband, the base and foundation of society, refuge of morals, defense of virtue, shield of innocence, protector of childhood, mirror of honor, axis of the family, and sole driver of civilization. It is undoubtedly a great and admirable thing to be a husband because you can spend your entire life sweetly entertained by envying those who are not married.

Very, very truly yours, from your true and impassioned admirer,

DIONISIO PÉREZ[73]

---

73. Dionisio Pérez Gutiérrez was a writer, journalist, and politician who often wrote about Spanish cuisine.

Friend Colombine:

My modest opinion cannot mean much in the debate on divorce that you so opportunely initiated. The matter is complex, and our society self-righteous; the admirable thing would be to examine the question from a physiological point of view without at all mixing in the issue of religion.

In our *Compilation of Laws*, there is one that was promulgated in 1385 by Don Alfonso in Segovia, which says, "Any woman who be wed with the words 'I do' with a man at least fourteen years of age, and she be at least twelve, and commit adultery, if the husband does find them in the act, *he may kill them both if he so wishes; therefore he may not kill one and leave the other and may kill both.*"

This brutal and ruthless conception of marriage is often manifested in modern Spanish society; this atavism persists, nourished by an education that relegates the development of one's volition to last place.

The Semitic, that is, the Hebrew or Arabian, blood of our ancestors enters as an interesting factor in the brutalities of destiny. While the Easterner hides the numerous slaves of his harem with a savage egoism, what won't we do to defend our one wife with rabid zeal?

On the other hand, no one has yet resolved the question of whether man is by nature monogamous or polygamous. Although a hypocritical modesty veils the truth, where is the individual, either single or married, who has not known more than one woman?

Difference in character is a sufficient reason to break off a marriage, as it means nothing but daily sacrifice and a hostility of constant pinpricks.

But, as a general rule, adultery is the cause that is seen as most serious, and no human or divine law can authorize a union to continue in these conditions.

There are women who fatally succumb to the blows of love without there having first been any dark complicity revealing a sensual passion. They are victims of a *surprise* as unexpected as an earthquake.

It evidences how slow our progress has been that we are still discussing such dark matters.

Well, Señora Colombine, you have had the honor of launching the seed to the winds of publicity; will it germinate one day? This hope gives encouragement not only to those who are married; we single men also trust that progress will do its work.

Life spreads, branches out, and extends; it is pointless to stop its movement, and in the chain of future generations, the effort of ideas, like the efforts of the material world, has its definitive triumph.

JOSÉ PÉREZ GUERRERO[74]

---

74. José Pérez Guerrero was a journalist and intellectual involved in several of Madrid's minor newspapers and weekly kiosk publications.

Friend Colombine:

When the invitation to take part in this *Trial* arrived in my alabaster hands, I found myself divorced of my good mood, and since at that moment Prisca Ruiz was there (the nursemaid who raised my youngest son), along with Vicentón the Simpleton,[75] to whom she was married—as God intended, according to the gossipers—it occurred to me to invite them over so they could advise in the matter. And so they said to me:

"You see, señorito," said Vicentón, "I don't know nothing about divorces, but if the couple didn't listen when they said, 'you better check the lot before you tie the knot,' for me if it's a bad marriage, they better figure it out and start living for each other. What I mean is, for the wife, if you know what I mean."

"This guy's right," added the nursemaid (a dry nurse now, so dry she was getting a bit crispy). "Either don't get married, that's the smart thing, or it's till death do us part, deal with it."

"So . . . if your Prisca does you wrong?" I asked Vicentón.

"I'd smash the first thing I could lay my hands on," the man answered.

"But would you keep on living with her?"

---

75. *Translator's note.* Vicentón el Chupacharcos, literally Vicentón the Puddle Slurper, a colorful way to describe a simpleton.

"Me? Ha! I'd get another girl. I'd rather have a cop!"

"But how can you say that, when earlier you were attacking divorce?"

"Come on! I was talking about other people. Because . . . I tell you, señorito: we didn't get hitched yet. God don't want us to get married in the church."

Which shows, dear Colombine, a lot of *sharp guys* break off their *conjugal relations* and walk the earth as they please. And obviously, since they were never married in the first place, they could give three licks about divorce.

Now, as for myself, I will tell you I vote in favor of divorce. But with these conditions: if the man is at fault, both spouses should be free to remarry, and additionally, a pension arising from the wife's work should be given to the husband. But if she is the one to blame, the man should kill her without any further thought. This way, as a general rule, we will obtain the separation of the spouses and freedom for the survivor.

If there are children, the matter is a bit more delicate, and I believe that if the parents truly love them, then on the day before the divorce, at nightfall, they should kill them too. This solution tends toward simplification of families and the avoidance of subsequent misery.

This, provocative Colombine, is the brilliant report I was able to send you—not, in the opinion of foreign authors, as inspired as others you may have received, but one that emerged spontaneously from this crumb of a brain that I put at your disposition.

Very truly yours,

JUAN PÉREZ ZÚÑIGA[76]

Señora Colombine:

Dear señora: Like many others, I find myself gripped by the desire to give my opinion on the matter of divorce.

Without a doubt we should remedy and prevent unhappy marriages, but, in my view, before we approve divorce, we should see to it that the bride and groom go to their marriage spontaneously, of their own free will, leaving behind paternal consent and advice, as well as the power of the parents to better the inheritance of certain children to the detriment of others, and the legal administration by the husband of the wife's assets.

I am certain that this reform will give a much better result than divorce.

CONSUELO DE REY[77]

---

76. Juan Pérez Zúñiga was a prolific writer, journalist, playwright, and humorist.

77. Consuelo de Rey y Fernández was the first teacher and director of Valencia's municipal music school for young girls, the Instituto Músico Público, which was created in 1868 as the first center to offer music studies to the public, including to families that could not otherwise afford them.

Señora Colombine:

In answer to your kind letter of the eighteenth of this month, I can only state that my opinion is contrary to the establishment of divorce in Spain.

FRANCISCO ROMERO ROBLEDO[78]

Señora Colombine:

My very esteemed and always admired and admirable friend: Late, excessively late, do I reply to your flattering invitation; I assure you I am not guilty of laziness, much less discourtesy; circumstances I will not torture you with—which, though I feared I would be late and hurtful, were more powerful than my firm will to quickly comply with the requirement of my very esteemed colleague—prevented me until today from telling you, since by the look of it you appear to want to know, my opinion on divorce.

My opinion (poor and unofficial since it is mine) can be expressed in a few words: I am resolved, decided and absolutely opposed to divorce.

---

78. Francisco Romero Robledo was a politician who opposed the abolition of slavery in the Spanish colonies of Puerto Rico and Cuba.

And not because I am a proponent of the indissolubility of marriage, but rather because marriage seems to me to be a bad sacrament and contract.

Very close to ten years have passed since I said, through a comedic character (because I have also perpetrated comedies—would you believe it, over twenty!), "What is divorce? A relic; progress traveling by cart; a back door out of marriage; let's get rid of marriage and we won't need divorce at all."

Since then up to now, my kind friend, I have not changed my mind; I continue believing today what I believed back then.

Each of us remembers events to suit our best interest, as the well-known saying goes, and to anticipate any assumptions by individuals who by nature are suspicious, I would like to point out that I was married civilly and religiously a good many years ago, and if there were such a thing as confirmation of marriage, I would remarry the woman that is my wife. And I would remarry her civilly, religiously, and even militarily if that became the fashion. You say there is an obvious contradiction between my opinion and my actions?

I believe there is one. Just as our lives are a continuous string of contradictions. I, the sincere and heartfelt enemy of immovable and irresponsible powers, contribute to sustaining immovable and irresponsible public officials.

The most hardened republican does not take a single step in public, or even in private, without accepting the monarchy. When the courts so desire, justice is meted out in the courts on behalf of the monarch, and any business is carried out and resolved by royal decree.

Enough of that; because when it comes to my private life and domestic satisfaction, they are only of interest to me and my family.

The words of Boileau which have been repeated so often over the past almost two-and-a-half centuries are as follows: *"Chassez le naturel, il revient au galop"*—more than the rule of a literary theorist, a legislator's maxim.[79]

To make marriage a contract is a veritable profanation, and more than that, it is reckless. Yet this is how it is! There may be husbands faithful to their wives, yes, sir! There may be some, but how few of them there are, if any!

I don't want to talk about wives, out of consideration for their sex. But, would I be saying something that everyone doesn't already know if I said that in the great capitals, same as in the small towns, as is known by everyone, there does indeed exist polygamy and even polyandry?

Well that's what happened; the law and customs tried to ignore Nature, and Nature prevailed.

And . . . I fear, esteemed friend, that if I continue down this path, I will slip since the path is slippery, and the topic

---

79. A French proverb meaning "a leopard cannot change its spots" (literally, "if you try to chase away your natural [character], it will come back galloping").

like a sheer cliff. Now you know my opinion on divorce; know also, I am your friend and admirer,

A. SÁNCHEZ PÉREZ[80]

Señora Colombine:

Dear señora: I received your letter and it would have been my pleasure to satisfy your wishes with an article for your *Diario*, except that I find myself in special circumstances forcing me to exercise extreme discretion in making sure my name occupies as little space as possible in the press.

Respectfully,

FRANCISCO SILVELA[81]

Señora Colombine:

Dear señora: You ask me about divorce, and I reply: I am single, and presently I aspire to marriage. How to aspire to divorce? If you want to ask me my legal, social opinion, and so on, I will tell you I am in favor of divorce.

---

80. Antonio Sánchez Pérez was a journalist, writer, and politician.

81. Francisco Silvela y de Le Vielleuze was a politician who held positions in various ministries. In 1903 he became president of the Council of Ministers and was later succeeded by Antonio Maura.

Therefore, it will not be long before I present a bill in Parliament that will allow all deputies to divorce if they so desire, if they approve the law first.

It seems to me that love, in many cases, is fleeting, a lightning bolt . . . and it is not about eternally condemning men and even women to the consequences of this spasm. For fires, there are water pumps and insurance companies. For the fire of Cupid, there should be an *Equitativa*,[82] and that is the *divorce law*.

Especially in Spain, where *matchmakers* and *feudal marriages of convenience* abound, always a pleasure . . . or not.

And where the children of Loyola act as go-betweens in what is a pleasure, stamping coins of love at the mint . . .

The marital bed, garden of love, should not become an abyss of hate. No natural, human, or divine law can hand down for the fickle crime of flirting the eternal sentence of forced marriage, along with a secondary sentence and legal expenses.

You might ask me about *the children and so on and so forth*. Ah! That is something that I, a single man, cannot resolve. What I can say is that there is no law, custom, or tradition that can impose *a legal union of two people separated by a divorce of the heart*. And divorce imposes itself in the case of this monstrous outrage.

---

82. A life insurance company, a branch of the Equitable Life Assurance Society of the United Kingdom.

And this without discussing the *tue-la* and other trivi-alities à la Dumas[83] that I resolve with the Toledan blade of the old Spanish theater.

The slave's shackles fell; the rights of man were born. Why shouldn't the claims of enslaved souls rise up from hearts thirsty for justice and true love?

Love, the richest, grandest thing in life, cannot be en-slaved and needs the expansion of divorce . . . *if justified*.

And if you ask my opinion of *divorce in general*, I will tell you that

I like all women

I like all women

in general

(I'm not talking about Linares[84]), and divorce for me is a done deal.

I'm divorced of the monarchists.

Divorced of some republicans.

Divorced of routine.

Divorced of parliamentary nonsense and all the "His Honor is so eloquent," and so on and so forth.

Divorced of all clerics, maybe even all organized religion . . .

Divorced of the Spanish *sanchopanzismo*,[85] tacky, ordi-nary, and vulgar.

---

83. Alexandre Dumas was a French novelist most famous for *The Three Musketeers* and other romantic tales of knights, sword battles, and adven-turous exploits.

84. A town in Andalusia.

85. Sancho Panza was Don Quixote's witty sidekick.

Divorced of everything.

Of everything, yes, except my family and a sweet Valencian thing that peeks out at the balcony amidst the sun's rays and the perfume of carnations, who has these black eyes that could fetter Alfred Naquet himself in the yoke of marriage.

RODRIGO SORIANO[86]

A lightning bolt that destroys, an earthquake that topples, even if they destroy and topple an ancient, crumbling building, have always caused me horror, just as I am horrified by divorce, which, because of an excess of pride or a triviality, can, in a moment of hysterical and unthinking excitement, destroy a palace of golden romance built by love after many years of constancy, affection, and appreciation. Without the hurricane wind of divorce—even if ruin were looming over this palace—when the efforts of the husband and wife are exhausted and they are convinced that rebuilding is impossible, they can still live happily, since for a nest, all one needs is a leafy tree or a crack in a large rock. Only those who feel humiliation or shame in this, instead of virtue and self-sacrifice, only for these people is the divorce law plausible, since, if it did

---

86. Rodrigo Soriano Barroeta-Aldamar was a republican politician, diplomat, and journalist known for his intense rivalries with Vicente Blasco Ibáñez and Alejandro Lerroux. He also dueled with three important military officers, including Primo de Rivera, who later became Spain's dictator.

not exist, it would have to be made into law to prevent a greater evil.

RAMÓN SURIÑACH BAELL[87]

Señora Colombine:

I should start by confessing that, despite being married, or maybe because of it, I've never managed to become interested in the question of divorce, nor have I been able to form my own opinion on the subject. The last thing I read about this matter—and I never read much about it—was on the parliamentary debate in the Argentine Republic, and what interested me much more than the question itself was the self-assured manner of speech, the richness of culture, the lofty tone that gives an excellent impression of that Parliament.

The same thing happens to me with divorce as with novels about adultery: they very rarely manage to interest me. I have always looked at everything regarding the relations between the sexes as subordinate to other kinds of matters. Therefore, feminism doesn't much capture my attention, considering that some of the issues it raises have to do with the organization and regulation of work and others having to do with general culture. The majority of the things women object to are things we men also experience.

---

87. Ramon Suriñach Baell was a Catalan playwright and poet.

Specifically, in terms of divorce, I have never been able to see the family as a mere union of husband and wife. Rather, and not to mention the children, I believe there is in marriage a relationship with society in general, which makes it a social institution and not a mere contract between spouses.

And it could be that divorce would bring greater harm to society if not for the subjection of those who marry to something greater, and to the family they create.

I also believe divorce is a weapon against women. I understand very well that many are fighting against marriage, whether as a religious sacrament or a civilly legalized contract, and the free union of man and woman is spreading, but I'm not doing a good job of explaining that this is about altering the nature of marriage. "Either fish or cut bait."

As you can see, my opinions in this regard are some of the most timid, the most backward, and the most bourgeois and least innovative. I recognize that, but I haven't managed to have other opinions.

Yours truly,

MIGUEL DE UNAMUNO[88]

---

88. Miguel de Unamuno y Jugo was an important Spanish novelist, poet, playwright, and philosopher who generally espoused liberalism.

Señora Colombine:

I apologize for being unable to write you by the date you indicated in your excellent letter, due to the infinite occupations in which I am enmeshed.

With pleasure do I use this opportunity to send you my respect and appreciation,

ANTONIO AGUILAR Y CORREA,[89]
Marquis of Vega de Armijo

Señora Colombine:

Dear señora: my health condition, which has been interrupting all my work, has prevented me from answering your kind letter and has, incidentally, made my opinion no longer timely.

Respectfully,

R. VILLAVERDE[90]

On Divorce

Marriage is possibly the only path to relative happiness that exists on earth. Who will not extol the benefits of it,

---

89. Antonio Aguilar y Correa was a politician and president of the Council of Ministers from 1906 to 1907.

90. Raimundo Fernández Villaverde was a politician who held various positions within the government of Alfonso XIII.

if they know them? To have at our side someone who understands us, a heart that beats in unison with ours, a disinterested friend who takes part in our happiness, or cries with us in our hours of pain; to make one life out of two; to struggle together when we have vigor and strength; to rest, also together, when old age comes; to sleep eternally under the same gravestone in the shadow of the same cross . . . is not all this the most serene and most beautiful future that two lovers can long for?

I even believe that at the side of our beloved, even hell itself can seem to be a place of joy. No one should consider themselves unfortunate if they can say, like Francesca da Rimini: *"Questi che mai da me non fia diviso."*[91]

If a marriage is based on such a foundation, and the spouses are bound by these ties, whether divorce exists matters little.

But such beauty is not always reality. It happens—all too often—that a marriage is born of a double lie. A young man and woman of marriageable age see and like each other: an engagement arises. The parents, looking after what they consider their material interests, which usually means no more than the economic situation of the couple, allow it. The fiancé is twenty-five years old; the fiancée, twenty. They don't know life; they don't know each other; maybe he confuses love and desire; maybe she sees in her wedding no more than the triumph of her vanity. In any

91. From Dante's *Inferno* 5.135: "This one, who ne'er from me shall be divided"; translation by Henry Wadsworth Longfellow, 1867; *Dante Lab Reader*, Dartmouth College, dantelab.dartmouth.edu/reader.

case, the wedding day arrives, and they commit to living united in an unbreakable bond until death.

Disenchantment usually comes quickly. The pretty woman, who seemed quite adorable during their visits, has become unbearable. The charming caballero in love, who seemed blessed during their engagement, has transformed into a brutal, crude, or impertinent man, or all three at once. And what is even sadder, they both see that they don't love each other. The mistake is obvious, but there is no recourse now. We can say in many cases that marriage is a trap we have fallen into.

> Once we have seen the trick
> and now we want to turn around,
> the way is blocked.

—

But these mistakes, although impossible to correct, are small potatoes, as the saying goes, compared to the extremely grave misfortunes caused by the indissolubility of marriage.

Before continuing, I should say that none of my observations on divorce refer to canonical marriage.

With respect to the *sacrament*, only the learned doctors of the Holy Mother Church have the proper jurisdiction over this very serious matter.

I'm talking strictly about earthly marriage here.

And with this caveat, I return to my topic.

How often do we see these youths whom mothers call "a good catch" simply because of the income or the rents they earn and who carry in their blood the seeds of terrible diseases acquired by sin! The case of Les avariés[92] is repeated with shocking frequency. Many of these men get married, and when their heinous affair or their inexcusable ignorance is discovered, the wife, now sick or in imminent danger of becoming sick, has no other recourse according to today's morals than to resign herself to "bearing her cross" and giving birth to children with rotten blood, condemned like Ibsen's Oswald[93] to imbecility or insanity or, in the best case, to a sickly, ailing existence. If the woman thus betrayed is horrified, not only by her own misfortune, but also by the idea of being a mother to miserable, ashamed descendants, and she rebels against such an absurd imposition, the unbreakable marriage chain binds her to commit a crime, one that is more shocking than to kill: the crime of giving life to children forced to live long, repugnant lives of suffering.

It also happens that love simply disappears and dies: the marriage becomes "the solitude of two together," as the poet said.[94] In this case, the husband's adultery almost always comes to light, and sometimes the wife's. And even if there is no spousal betrayal, wouldn't it always turn the stomach of a delicate soul, the idea of giving or

---

92. A 1901 play (Damaged Lives in English) by Eugène Brieux. It was banned for dealing with syphilis.

93. A character from The Ghosts (1882) who is believed to have inherited syphilis from his father (although it is now established that syphilis is not transmitted this way).

94. "La soledad de dos en compañía." From Ramón de Campoamor, Las tres cosas: Dichas sin nombre (pequeños poemas), Francisco Álvarez, 1886, p. 7.

receiving kisses from lips that one imagines may land on a mouth other than the one that they kiss so coldly and with a pained sense of duty.

How many such evils, such betrayals, such deceit, and such infidelity could be corrected with divorce, thus recognizing the absolute sovereignty of love, the only tie that can indeed bind souls!

—

"Oh! What about the children?" they exclaim, the enemies of divorce, taking refuge in their last trench. "Marriage," they say, "must continue to be indissoluble for their sake. How are they to blame for the antagonism of their parents? If the parents separate, what will be the fate of the children?"

Aside from the fact that the offspring have been provided for by law in countries where there is divorce, we should not ignore the fact that a marriage that is ruptured, for whatever reason, is much worse for the children than a divorce.

Can a house where there is betrayal and lies, where there is fighting and no affection, be a place for raising children? Can love and respect for their parents take root in them when they see hostility, mutual distrust, and disrespect?

I remember few scenes as tremendous as a scene from the novel *Trivialities*,[95] in which the children of Currita Albornoz, hiding, see how the adulterers *adorn* the portrait of

---

95. *Pequeñeces* (1891), by Luis Coloma.

Villamelón, painting the undignified sign of his shame on his forehead. Whatever the fate of those children would be if their parents were to divorce, wouldn't it be better than the disillusionment of their most holy affections and the corruption of their innocence?

—

Strictly speaking, there does exist for men, if not legal divorce, a certain kind of divorce tolerated by custom. Deceitfully or openly, the husband who has fallen out of love goes elsewhere to seek, and sometimes find, the love that has escaped his home. But for the wife, the escape hatch of divorce being closed off to her, she has only one of two paths to choose: either sacrifice for the rest of her life or the shame of adultery.

ZEDA[96]
(From *La Época*)

Señora Colombine:

Another opinion on divorce? Ah, beautiful and very eloquent friend! This should not worry either you or me personally. We don't deserve to be abandoned suddenly. As regards people who are already de facto divorced, what does it matter if the law confirms what reality has already declared to be irremediable?

---

96. Francisco Fernández Villegas, also known as Zeda, was a journalist, playwright, translator, theater critic, and fiction writer.

Should divorce exist or not? I don't know, but it exists. What we have is that according to the twenty-fourth session of the Council of Trent, "If anyone saith that the bond of matrimony may be dissolved, etc., etc., *let him be anathema*."

Well, we'll say it, in private. Divorce has always existed, the divorce of minds, feelings, bodies, and souls. In more than a few conjugal beds, the sleepers are separated by worlds of revulsion. Today, as before, faithfulness continues to be a characteristic feature of . . . men? No, of dogs. Today, as in the time of Diocletian, it is rare to find a woman's gravestone where it would be right to say *inclitæ, univiræ.*[97]

My transcendentalism is sleeping the sleep of my candor. How can I believe that the laws can be other than what is dictated by life? The law does no more than declare social facts. Divorce is a fact. It is therefore beneficial to declare it. Standing before our false modesty is the sovereign immanence[98] of things. We have a code that impedes married people from entering into a new union, but the thing is, this code is not obeyed. Opposite the *homo non separet* is the supreme law of love, the essence and nature of which is free.

---

97. *Inclitæ* is Latin for "illustrious women." *Univiræ* (from *unus* ["one"] and *vir* ["man"]) means "women who are monogamous for life." *Univiræ* originally referred to a select group of women, such as the wives of priests who worshipped Jupiter. It only came to mean monogamous women in general during the Christian period, well after the reign of Diocletian.

98. *Translator's note. Inmanente* means, roughly, inherent to something or united to it in a way that is inseparable from its essence, although it may be rationally distinguished.

I can imagine the scandal this will produce among the militant Tartuffes.[99] As for me, the demand that all married couples love each other and remain united in body and soul produces the same effect as this decree of a chemist: "Starting today, there will be no elective affinities. Lime will always be from carbonic acid, and from sulfuric acid, potash." Everything will go quite well until we put the four components in contact with each other. "What will be of the children if we allow divorce?" Madame Duval asks in *Le dédale*.[100] The question seems to deeply worry all the modern French playwrights, who have been trying these past twenty years to find an excuse for adultery. What will be of the children? It appears that today, for the children of those who are de facto divorced, the issue has already been resolved. The drunk, brutish lout of a husband squanders his assets, neglects his children's upbringing, tortures the children with his cruelty, and perverts them with his example. The imbecile, the adulteress, forgets them, prostitutes them, and abandons them. Where is there a greater sorrow for a child than to witness their parents' covert fighting every day? A greater, sadder misfortune than for a child to see hate, betrayal, desperation, or unbearable agony in the faces of those who gave them life. We are left with feeding and clothing the child. But is there a law that denies this to a child once the fiery maelstrom is over, which is

---

99. Main character from Molière's play *Tartuffe* (1664), whose name was synonymous with being a religious hypocrite.

100. A play by Paul Hervieu, which premiered in December 1903.

more odious than that of Francesca and Paolo,[101] since in this case the damned couple, instead of embracing each other, bite and spit at each other and tear each other to bits.

The enemies of divorce invoke the dignity of the woman. But precisely the same people who want to dignify her by subjecting her to a barbaric slavery declare that she is incapable of any noble function—the priesthood, the judiciary bench, or higher education—or even parental authority, which only the revolution could give her. The woman is horrifying to the ascetic, a source of evil in primitive fiction, and seduction and contagion for those who make their best vows in seclusion. Dignify the woman! She is only dignified in emancipation, if she becomes sui juris, not subjected to eternal guardianship, constant censure, and submission and everlasting passivity.

Sad defense of a law that prevents divorce for a woman who is scorned, injured, and abandoned by her spouse! If a dignified woman is not able to keep the father of her children by her side, she should want him to leave. But he should leave for good, to suffer in anguish without consolation, in isolation among crowds, the shame of his own failure.

Keep him in the house? For what? To comment on *doloras* and measure the horror of *the solitude of two together*?[102] For a man whose honor was cunningly offended, the best

101. Francesca da Rimini and Paolo Malatesta, adulterers in Dante's *Inferno*.
102. *Translator's note. Dolora* refers to a short poetic composition of dramatic spirit, which encapsulates a reflection. The quotation is the one by Ramón de Campoamor cited in note 94.

thing he can do is separate himself forever from someone who cannot give him affection, consolation, kindness, or mercy. To kill is savage; to forgive is impossible. Children don't need impure mothers.

Indissoluble marriage would be very beautiful . . . if it existed. It is the first opposition, a most intimate, sexual one, and the man and his woman live together in it like a single superior individual for purposes of carrying out the human functions. Even so, there *is* a case where the two halves of Franklin's scissors should separate: if together, they no longer cut.[103]

Let's be sincere: let's bring custom into law; let's not try to create fictitious universes from the tripod.[104] Divorce exists; the law must manage it. Let us not be horrified by the danger of it. Free to break their commitments, or not to, few men will feel strong enough to abandon the treasure that today, because of a sense of security in their possession, they look at with indifference. Faced with the remotest fear of losing the affection of the women who have honored and elevated us, uniting their adorable hands with ours—how many of us rebels would bend the knee!

---

103. Benjamin Franklin wrote, in a 1787 letter to a friend, "[A]fter all, wedlock is the natural state of man. A bachelor is not a complete human being. He is like the odd half of a pair of scissors, which has not yet found its fellow, and, therefore, is not even half so useful as they might be together"; *Memoirs of Benjamin Franklin; Written by Himself*, edited by Steven Gibbs and Richard J. Shiffer, vol. 2, Harper and Brothers, 1860; *Project Gutenberg*, 2012, www.gutenberg.org.

104. Referring to the three-legged bench used in antiquity for divination, such as the one used by the oracle of Delphi.

And out of every one hundred unshackled men, ninety—and don't you doubt it, oh, big soul!—will return to their warm corner of love, trembling, and shout to the sad, melancholy figure: My fairy, wife, mother, companion! Liberty is you!

Very, very truly yours, Doña Carmen de Burgos Seguí, distinguished writer. Your very affectionate admirer,

ANTONIO ZOZAYA[105]
(From *El Liberal*)

---

105. Antonio Zozaya You was a prolific journalist who wrote mostly for *El Liberal* and *La Libertad*. He was also a fiction writer and jurist and a founder of the Republican Left political party in 1934. After the Spanish Civil War, he fled to France, where his two daughters and daughters-in-law ended up in concentration camps. He fled to Mexico, where he died.

Part Two: Opinions of Readers

Señora Colombine:

Dear esteemed señora: In "Readings for Women," which *Diario Universal* published, I read a news item that was much more sensational than Maeztu's article opposing the centenary of *Quixote*—much more sensational.*

It was this news item that says that a Club of Unhappily Married Couples will be forming to request the establishment of divorce in Spain.

The idea seems so excellent to me that I feel compelled to say to you—good God!—please keep your numerous readers apprised of this matter, because I know of a few señoras that would go with their heads held high to take part in this society, to achieve what women in other countries have achieved, that is, to avoid seeing themselves tyrannized, not by a man, but by something worse, by a contract, which, when you get down to it, is what marriage is.

And in effect, when this contract cannot be carried out *in full*, because one of the *contracting parties* cannot or

---

* This letter and the article by D. Francisco Durante gave rise to this plebiscite.

does not want to carry it out, then what is left between them? A life of endless sorrow, which could be remedied by another union, in which they would fulfill the goals of moral and material existence.

Because, as you know very well, Señora Colombine, there are many unhappy and separated couples. If the man who is separated has found a woman who loves him, he cannot get close to her—this hypocritical society will label him as soon as possible as a frivolous man. And if on the contrary, it is a separated woman who loves another man, because she cannot and must not love her husband—ah!—then she is undignified and repudiated by everyone, when she has committed no crime except to love, which is one of the goals of our lives, and maybe one of the main ones.

If it seems to you that these lines are publishable, since you do so much for women, I beg you, please publish them, asking your readers to give their opinions on this matter, of vital interest for women, and you should know, Señora Colombine, that if at this moment I do not give my name, it is because I fear I would soon be criticized. But I am sure that once one woman starts to lay out her ideas on this matter, many others will follow suit. I will postpone giving my name until then.

In the meantime, I beg you to give life and support in *Diario Universal* to everything related to the creation of the Club, and soon your best admirer will have the pleasure of greeting you in person. Sincerely,

C. V. DE P.

The Divorce Club

The news item published in *Diario Universal* regarding the probable formation of a Club of Unhappily Married Couples to request the establishment of divorce has fallen among the señoras like May showers on land thirsty for beneficent rain. . . .

But we are not talking about the illusory divorce allowed by the Church and our civil code, which consists of separation of the spouses. It is about something much more momentous: what we could call the legal termination of the marriage contract, by which the two contracting parties have the absolute freedom to remarry or, to be more precise, to enter into a new contract.

But I didn't think all of this would make it past the threshold of the feminist ideal in our country, and since feminism is a pleasant sport, and nothing more than a sport, the project would float like a remote hope in the souls of unhappy couples and people easily swayed by novelty.[106]

This was my assumption, thinking about the superior place occupied by marriage in Spain compared to other countries, a superior place rooted in our women's self-denial, in their faithfulness and sweet, traditional resignation, which has given them, in my view, a certain stamp of grandeur.

---

106. The word "sport" is in English in the Spanish text.

But what I have here is that these same women are beginning to realize that marriage is a cruel contract. Guidance to this effect comes from outside Spain. A woman in France can be unmarried and then remarry. Why shouldn't the same thing happen here? And desire, which usually has lighter wings than reason, has manifested itself openly, bravely, by señoras in the columns of this very newspaper.

I have many reservations, and for the record, more than a few words of warning, not so much regarding the request for divorce, which doesn't scare me, but regarding the basis for the petition, because it destroys something very spiritual, very beautiful in the minds of our youths, something that has the delicate nuances of an honorable Romanticism.

For these fresh, happy minds, disenchantment is great. There is more than one love? Doesn't there exist only one single love that brings man and woman to the foot of the altar? Well, if love brought them there, how does it die, and how can another equal one be born, also subject to such an ending?

The theory of divorce has this cold, unconsoling note for me. Byron says, "'Tis just six years since we were one, and five since we were two." But is that true, spiritually? The woman, married for love, divorces and remarries, in love? Did she love twice, or is it that she did not love at all?

A woman who separated from her husband because their characters were incompatible (or for more serious reasons) continues loving him in spite of herself, unable to find the willpower to stop. And I have met many men who find themselves in the same boat. But these are men who married for love.

The señoras who ask for a divorce so they can remarry, did they love their husbands? That is what I wonder. They married without loving each other and didn't realize it, or they did realize it and married anyways. Unfortunately, the two cases are all too common for both men and women.

Next, not even dealing exclusively with these extremes, I will explain desire. Has the marriage been so bad, so bad that you are forced to undo it? Why get remarried when you will only expose yourself to the same thing? I have never seen anyone hit with a club beg for more.

No, I don't think it is right that love should serve as a pretext to support the request for divorce. The true reason, the only one by the way, is the total absence of love. Let it be born, let it grow and take root before you get married, and you will see it will be impossible to free yourselves of its influence, whether good or bad.

An esteemed señora said in the pages of *Diario Universal* that "love is one of the goals of our lives." Exactly. But is marriage an impediment to love or is it a consecration of love itself?

And for the record, I am not defending marriage as a goal, not even as a means to an end. I am defending logic. And I sincerely believe that divorce, precisely as it has been established in France, is the first step toward the philosophical conclusions of Sébastien Faure: "All the elderly are our parents; all the children are our children."[107]

Are you seduced by theory? Well it is through theory that we have something called free love, but I have not managed to figure out how two such fundamentally contradictory concepts like love and freedom can be together—I always took love for a tyrant over the will, which subjugates and enslaves the lover.

Señoras and señores of the Divorce Club, the thing is that desire, I repeat, has very long, light wings. Before we arrive at divorce, in effect, which resolves the situation of those that have not loved, wouldn't it be logical to democratize our customs and get to the point of not fooling each other?

Women have a special knack for hiding their flaws before marriage. And the same is true of men. But the curious thing is that the instant they are married, neither the man nor the woman feels obligated to conceal these flaws. And this constitutes a serious evil.

We need to get used to thinking the same thing in public as in private, and to reason with the same bravery when people are listening and when they are not, amen to banishing from our minds the idea of marriages for convenience.

Nothing more in defense of love; it's smooth sailing from here on out, which wouldn't have been the case in

---

107. Faure was a French anarchist. However, this quote is rightfully attributed to the French anarchist poet Paul Paillette and is found in his 1887 work *Les Enfants de la Nature*.

defense of marriage or against termination of the contract. It is possible that my radicalism in this matter and a few others goes beyond that of the founders of this club. But I will not explain it because I do not want it said that a transgression of my pen was to blame if the *let him be anathema* were to fall on the shoulders of *Diario Universal*.

FRANCISCO DURANTE[108]

You say, Señora Colombine, when you insert the letter of Doña C. V. de P. regarding the Club of Unhappily Married Couples, that you will let the public know the opinion of your women readers on this delicate topic.

Only women readers? Not men? Don't we men form at least half of the married couple? I believe you are impartial and fair, so I will dare bother you, and your readers if you will, with these lines, which should be a few, although I could speak very much about the *delicate* matter.

First, the statements of Señora de P. seem very correct. We need something more than the separation of assets and bodies: we need divorce in Spain if we are to *Europeanize*. Not too long ago, a French lady said to me that we Spaniards are Turks with our women (without a doubt she meant savages), that we imprison them, that they live without freedom, etc., etc.

---

108. Francisco Durante was a journalist and columnist whose letter to Burgos inspired her plebiscite on divorce.

I told her about the case of a friend of mine who, fifteen days after he got married, was left without a wife because the weather in Madrid didn't suit her, and she wanted to return to the town where she was born. The husband protested, but she left (first act of the drama *The Married Woman's Freedom*). He wrote letters and more letters; his life's sweet companion refused to return to their marriage bed (second act). The husband was tired and called the authorities; then the wife, angry at this incredible tyranny, returned, but . . . eight days later, she turned the house of her guardian upside down (third act).

Again my friend beseeched the authorities to help him, and they said to him, "Man, you can't change your wife. Tell her to take a hike!" Could we possibly give more freedom to a married woman, who is considered a *minor* according to the law, and a more *minor status* to the married man? Do we Spaniards treat our wives like savages?

My friend lives alone; his wife, before God and men, has abandoned him, has undone his home, and has denied him a family. Is it fair for this man to be condemned to live the way he lives? And if he doesn't live like this and does create a new family (I won't even mention the gossiping), this man can be sent to prison by his *legal wife*.

Ah! It is true what the French lady said to me: we Spaniards are Turks, savages, but it's because we submit to preposterous, tyrannical laws.

Canalejas, who talks so much about the religious orders—it wouldn't be bad if he talked about establishing divorce in our country, which is more important than the expulsion of the orders. And I stress that I said *more* important.

Señora, I am married, my wife has read these lines, we are happy, and she agrees with me because she is convinced that what joins two people forever are their souls and not imposed ties, convenience, or unconsciousness dressed up in sacred formulas. And believe me, if one day our souls cannot be united like they are today, she and I will come and join the Club, to ask, shouting loud, for the independence of the body and spirit, now imprisoned in social conventions and stale ideas that are a slap to civilization.

Respectfully,

JUAN PÉREZ

Señora Colombine:

I'm not sure who this sincere C. V. de P. is, but of course I can guess she was not born to be a woman, nor does she deserve to be one.

Obviously, I am referring to the passionate supporter of divorce, who wants everyone to pay the price for her misconduct, or his, whatever the case may be.

Doesn't it seem to the señora and to you, who support her, that these things, even if they are right, should never be put forward by a woman, because if she has not forgotten about her sex, which is called to the highest purpose and the loftiest virtues, she should possess forbearance, and if she is disgraced, she should carefully keep her mistakes quiet if she is guilty, so that she does not lose her upright reputation, which it would behoove her more to circulate, since private honor and modesty have been so abused.

The women and men, everyone who asks for divorce—the men are either fools or neurasthenics and the woman hysterical, or else they are all depraved individuals who deserve to be rebuked so that—since they do not contribute one iota of kindness and purity to society—they at least do not insert themselves into our public places, with scandal, and even with the carelessness they learned in school, the virus of a subtle and truly abhorrent prostitution.

Señora Colombine, these things should not be published; it reveals, at the least, a lightness that, in you who are friendly, is excusable, but it is not healthy.

I already know that these lines will not appear in *Diario Universal*, for the same reason that if one speaks the truth and upholds the ancient principles of our past morality, it injures the pride of some women, and—ah!—this and exhibition are things that feminist *theory* places above everything: above the home, the parents, the love of the children, everything.

DARÍA BÜNSEN

Señora Colombine:

As the noteworthy columnist Señor Durante says very well in his article "The Divorce Club," the creation of this club "has fallen among the señoras like May showers on land thirsty for beneficent rain." That is perfectly true, my respectable Señora Colombine. But as the exquisite writer has a few doubts, let me see if I can respond to his questions so the doubts disappear.

I'll start by stating that the letter of the señora C. V. de P. seems admirable for its sincerity and courage, which lifts the spirits of women so we can come out of our discouragement and dejection, which we are now in the process of coming out of, and people should listen to us.

Yes, Señor Durante: this is what it is about. It is about the "termination of the marriage contract," since it is a contract, and the *only one* that lasts in perpetuity. It's not that desire has more wings than reason; it is that desire is forged on the anvil of necessity, and it is an aspiration that has given everyone, men and women, a long and very painful experience. And if the foundation of the divorce petition destroys something very spiritual, very beautiful in young minds and their honorable Romanticism, what does all this matter if one comes to conquer a relative happiness that exists in this world?

Is there more than one love? the delicate columnist asks. I can't tell you, nor does it matter in the end. But I will say that men and women do not get married because *one single* love brings them to the foot of the altar. How is it that another love is born and dies? Ah! Señor Durante, how is it that the flowers on a single rosebush are born, die, and are reborn? In our hearts, our feelings are renewed in this way, and if we love our parents, then our spouses, then our children, and then we lose some of them, and then more and more of them, and our wounds are healed, and we even come to forget what we once thought was unforgettable.

If we are married for *one* single love, how do widows and widowers get married for the second time? Your psychology is incomprehensible when you say that women, separated from their husbands for having committed grave offenses, continue loving them. No, as much as they may hold them in high esteem, they do not love them, because if they did they would not have committed these grave offenses. We señoras that ask for divorce, we *have* been able to love our husbands, but what if they have become unworthy of our love? And what if they, with their mistresses, have profaned more than the conjugal home, and the blindfold has fallen from our eyes, and we have recovered our dignity? What should we do then? Resign ourselves? Be quiet? Kiss the hand of the master that whips us? Are you lovers of liberty, and yet for us women you want a loathsome slavery that is repugnant to any honorable conscience? There are many, an infinite number, of women who go to marriage loving their husbands, but there are many who go to it not loving them, because here in Spain, you men have taught us to believe that the only career for women is marriage, and the woman has found her modus vivendi[109] in it. Love, you are right, is a tyrant over the will, but what about when there is no love? But let's say that you do go to marriage with love, in good faith, remember the words of Madame de Staël[110]: "Marriage is the tomb of love." Also remember the words of Byron, since you quote him: "Marriage is a sack full of serpents and one eel; he who grabs the eel is happy."[111] Well, divorce is not for the one who picked the eel; it is for the ones that picked the serpents.

"To democratize our customs" until we get to the point of not mutually fooling ourselves. Is that all! That is the ideal. But how do we get to this point? By a long series of generations that progress in moral and intellectual education. In synthesis, Señor Durante: there may be love in marriage, but there may not be. In the case where there isn't love, divorce is an admirable and *essential* institution—with it, the spouses push aside reprehensible and repugnant things: betrayal and cheating. Isn't loyalty preferable?

---

109. *Translator's note.* In Spanish and English, *modus vivendi* often refers to often temporary political arrangements between conflicting parties. In Spanish, however, it has the additional meaning of "a way to make a living" or "livelihood."

110. Anne Louise Germaine de Staël-Holstein. The quotation should be attributed to Giacomo Casanova, *History of My Life*, translated by William Trask, Johns Hopkins UP, 1967, p. 208.

111. Lord Byron may have quoted this line, but the original quotation is from Thomas More: "I have herde my father meryly say every man is at the choyce of his wife, that ye sholde put your hande into a blynde bagge full of snakes and eles together, vii snakes for one ele"; *A Dialogue of Syr Thomas More, Knyghte*, London, 1557, p. 165; book 1 of *The Workes of Sir Thomas More Wrytten in the Englysh Tonge.*

To the señora Doña Daría Bünsen, I must say that C. V. de P. is a woman and was born to be one. Why should a woman not propose a measure that could be a lifesaver to so many others? If this señora has been wronged, she should keep quiet; why? No, on the contrary, she should say so, because such misfortune is a good way to sink into an abyss, and if one has sunk into it, she should at least have the excuse of her misfortune. "We need to get used to thinking the same thing in public as in private." If the señora de P. is to blame and not the one who was wronged, her misery is great, but we must admit that she is wise to advocate for the establishment of divorce, precisely for this reason, so that she can stop being to blame. Yes, those of us who ask for, who clamor for, divorce must be neurasthenics, but don't call us hypocrites who, clothed in piety, are hiding the odious sin of betraying our vows.

So there you go, Señora Colombine, my name and address, hoping as you say, you will protect my name from the public.

Warm regards,

DOLORES FERNÁNDEZ

Since I believed it to be a joke, Señora Colombine, the letter published the twenty-eighth of last December in *Diario Universal* by a señora who reveals herself to be strongly in favor of the creation of a Club of Unhappily Married Couples, I did not write to you that same day; but after reading the noteworthy article of Señor Durante, who seems to have taken it seriously, I can do no less than beg all my fellow countrywomen to express their opinions on this matter, of such capital interest to the Spanish woman.

So I will start with my own example, saying that I am completely in agreement with the authoritative viewpoint of Señor Durante, and I would only add that divorce destroys, along with morals and religion, the family, and as such, society. It also does not much advance true feminism, and in terms of women's dignity, it is very damaging. Regarding the extremely sad situation of the poor children, I won't go into that here so that tears won't burst from the beautiful eyes of my sensible readers.

I won't deny there are husbands with whom life is unbearable; it is also evident that some wives turn their homes into a hell; but when this occurs, it seems better to me that, armed with patience, self-sacrifice, and tolerance, we await with resignation until God decides to cut the marriage bond with the death of one of the spouses.

It is not possible for a woman to find happiness at the side of another man after having annulled the marriage with the father of her children, before whom she must feel small because of the degrading anathemas that the majority of people will hurl at her.

I am secure in the fact that Spanish señoras will once again reveal their illustriousness, reason, and good judgment, energetically protesting the formation of the Club of Unhappily Married Couples; with their cultural education and good sense of life experience, it cannot be hidden from them that divorce is a direct attack on morals and religion, it lessens their dignity, and the mother will have to blush whenever the innocent eyes of her children look at her; to avoid this shame, they will bravely suffer the indignities of their marriages and they will not want to hypocritically conceal their vices with the advantages given to them by divorce.

I will not end my letter without sending you, Señora Colombine, my most sincere congratulations on the good advice this newspaper gives to mothers on childrearing; if they follow that advice, they will surely find such pleasure, with the affection and joy of their little ones, that they will not occupy themselves with other loves, if unfortunately they are not happy with their husbands.

I send you my greetings and warmest regards,

FARINATA
Ciudad Rodrigo, 2 January 1904

Señora Colombine:

My opinion is one of the most enthusiastic ones in favor of divorce.

ADOLFA GABAN

Yesterday we published a letter from one of our readers in favor of divorce. Today we received another one against this idea, and since it fulfilled our requirement of revealing the person's name and address, we rushed to publish it.

Does this not prove our impartiality?

However, neither this nor my own formal intention of not giving my modest opinion until I write the summary frees me from criticism.

They say women and clerics are not considered discourteous if they turn their back on one in public. Well, a good señor, not a woman, has turned his back to me, bitterly criticizing me in a bland, incoherent, and grotesque article in *Revista Benéfica Española*.

What the good señor *marquess of Siete Picos* says to me—and that's a lot of picos![112]—is so lacking in inventiveness that I wouldn't normally bother to respond except to point out the injustice of it, given that I have not yet stated my opinion.

We are just having a discussion, and as is well known, "from discussions come light." Is it that the señor de Picos is scared of this light?

Come now, a little bit of logic (though he doesn't know French, as we can see) is always beneficial to someone who would take the *modest* pseudonyms *Troubadour of the Virgin* or the *Cantor of Guadarrama!*

---

112. *Translator's note.* A classic novel by Pedro A. de Alarcón is titled *El sombrero de tres picos* (*The Three-Cornered Hat*). This hat was a symbol of power because it was worn by a corregidor, a local authority. Siete Picos is a mountain in the Sierra de Guadarrama range near Madrid. Burgos is joking that this man must think he is quite important, since his title refers not to a three-cornered hat but to a seven-peaked mountain—*pico* means both a hat corner and a mountain peak.

But leaving all this aside, since this is about divorce, let's see what our colleague at *El Globo* said yesterday: "A current of public opinion is beginning to form in Spain in favor of divorce."

Asked yesterday on the timeliness and effectiveness of this campaign, a political personage answered dryly: "*Divorce* was established here a long time ago."

"How?"

"Simple: We are *divorced* from the country, and the country from us. The government is *divorced* from public opinion, and public opinion from it. Valencia is *divorcing* Nozaleda,[113] and that's it. The entire nation is in an unhappy marriage."

COLOMBINE
Response to an insert in
Revista Benéfica Española

This subject, Señora Colombine, is getting a lot of play, and we must thank you for your independence and bravery in addressing this issue of such burning interest since the fate of many hinges on it, and this is a matter that demands resolution.

I am very enthusiastically following what the señoras and caballeros are saying about divorce, and I will make a statement for you: I am a single woman because divorce

---

113. See note 18.

does not exist among us. No matter how maturely one thinks things through, one may make a mistake, and to ask one who *made an agreement for life* to be resigned to the mistake is too much to ask. This, since obviously it is preposterous, there is no need to discuss, but yes, we should discuss what Farinata said, because what others have said has already been answered, and very well in my opinion, by Dolores Fernández.

Farinata assures us that divorce destroys the family, morals, and religion. It wouldn't hurt if she gave evidence of that, but let me see if I can give some evidence to the contrary.

The family is not destroyed if divorce exists, just as it hasn't been destroyed in France, England, Germany, Austria, Russia, Belgium, etc., etc., and "the extremely sad situation of the poor children" is less extremely sad in a *calm home* with the warmth of love than in a home where they see the discord of the parents, their mutual lack of respect, and something else, what all this leads to when two people do not love each other and *are forced* to live together, to servilely submit, after insults, to the odious tyranny of the flesh. This is immoral! And also it is much more moral to live *legally* with the person one loves than to wish for the death of the person one abhors, awaiting "with resignation until God decides to cut the marriage bond with the death of one of the spouses!" What horror!

Why would a divorced woman have any reason to blush in front of her children! Does a widow who is remarried blush in front of the children whose father is deceased?

I believe I have demonstrated that neither the family nor our morals suffer with the establishment of divorce, and in terms of religion, I don't know one other than Catholicism, nor would I want to, but when it comes to such a momentous issue as divorce, and when religion gets thrown into the ring saying it is offended and destroyed, it would be good for women to know what our most illustrious holy fathers of the Catholic Church have to say about us.

It is known that at the synod of Mâcon, the question of whether women have a *soul* was debated with the utmost gravity.

Saint John Chrysostom says that "woman is but an enemy of friendship, a necessary evil, a domestic danger." These are the words of Saint Jerome: "Woman is the road of iniquity and the sting of a scorpion." Do you want more, my dear colleagues? Well, we can cite innumerable other *compliments* from the holy fathers, who say that apparently we want to *continue* to be enslaved in marriage in order to prove the venerable saints right, to *continue* being a domestic danger and scorpion sting for the poor little husband.

Maybe we women have much to thank the church fathers for—let's figure out a way to stand up for ourselves a little and stop being such *a domestic danger.*

In conclusion, Señora Colombine, I recall the words of Saint Teresa of Jesus: "Hell is a place where there is no love." And hell can exist for a married couple in perpetuity, and love for a divorced and remarried one, since the marriage contract is but a certificate of the dignity and honor of love.

ESPERANZA CASTRO

Señora Colombine:

Dear señora: Having read the letter that was published last night in *Diario Universal*, and understanding that its author is not in favor of the Club of Unhappily Married Couples and that it seems she wants to give us a moral lesson in her letter, it seems to me a good idea to protest a few things she writes in it.

Farinata says that divorce destroys morals, religion, the family, and society and that women's dignity is damaged. And she advises us that we should arm ourselves with patience, self-sacrifice, and tolerance until God decides to sever the tight bond of marriage with the death of one of the spouses. Stop right there! I protest, I protest from the bottom of my heart, and I believe the same will be done by those women who have found nothing but heartache and misery since the day they were engaged.

I am also not in agreement with another little paragraph of Farinata's, which says that a woman cannot be happy with another man after having annulled the marriage with the father of her children. Why not? If from the moment she separates from her husband she stops suffering! Why would the children look down at their mother, if they are good children and don't see any objectionable behavior in her? And why would we think that the woman uses divorce to hypocritically conceal her vices? Why do we need to condemn an unhappy wife if she wants to do whatever she can to break her bond to the man who is the cause of all her misfortunes?

Also, not every woman has children, and also, unfortunately for society, there are many couples that marry for convenience, and sometimes the convenience of the parents, without the daughter feeling any affection toward the man with whom she will unite. And if on top of that, the husband does not love her, what is marriage to the woman? Well, if there is no divorce, she is miserable and there is no salvation whatsoever. Of course it's true, if she has children it is a consolation, but we need to open our eyes: having children will not take away all of a woman's suffering.

Also—and I believe nobody knows this better than a mother—if she, even with all the affection of her children, decides to separate from her husband, she must have her reasons, and it is well known that no mother ever stops having a soul.

Believe me, Señora Colombine, the author of this letter published on Friday must be a señorita, who, swayed by the words of her fiancé, and feeling the rush of first love in her heart, has allowed herself to be carried away by her feelings, ignoring the fact that no matter how virtuous a woman may be, there are sufferings in an unhappy marriage that make her forget her duties as a wife and almost her duties as a mother.

My opinion is that any woman who is not happy in her marriage and who has self-esteem and dignity must want divorce to be established in Spain.

Finally, I want to say viva the Club of Unhappily Married Couples and anyone who makes efforts toward that end.

As a subscriber to this newspaper, and sincerely feeling everything I have said here, I have dared write to you and give you my opinion.

Yours sincerely,

CLARA Y.

To Colombine:

I have in front of me a story of divorce written by a notable man of letters, and from this interesting reading I gather that societies that are distinguished by their barbarism and that consider marriage to be a contract have established divorce; in all of them arbitrariness and injustice reigns, it always ends up causing harm to the women and children, and I don't see advantages for society, the family, or the government.

Let's consider divorce from a religious perspective. We all know marriage was instituted by the Lord, first as a contract between Adam and Eve, when they enjoyed the delights of paradise; later Jesus Christ raised marriage to the level of a sacrament when he came to the world to preach the Christian religion. It is, therefore, a contract and a sacrament to us, with the three conditions of the latter being *unity, indissolubility, and legitimacy.*

It is evident that the indissolubility of marriage rests in the nature of God, man, and civil society. It is one of the traits of the divine family of the Holy Trinity, a type of human family.

When uniting our first parents, God said to Adam, "I give you this companion, who is flesh of your flesh," indicating that man and woman are two in one, indivisible and inseparable. This is what Jesus Christ said later to the Pharisees: "Let no man separate what God has joined together."

In the Council of Trent, church leaders agreed that neither the husband nor the wife could contract a new marriage as long as one of the spouses was still alive.

Saint Paul and other luminaries of the Catholic Church have the same opinion.

We also don't have to make a great effort of imagination to understand that the family is destroyed with the separation of the individuals that form it; the children follow one of the spouses, or maybe some follow the mother and others the father, but in any case, they lose the care of one parent, and the affection of the absent parent always diminishes, so they receive a poorer upbringing than if they had lived with both.

If the spouses do not have love in perpetuity, they will love each other less and will not please each other. And the woman will make laws of her most minimal impulses; if the husband does not obey, she will impose these laws on another, and another, but when she loses her beauty and youth, she will fall into the most horrible slavery, being left in the end, without a family, maybe without a home, seeing herself deprived of the respect and consideration that virtue deserves.

Meanwhile, divorce has become law in Catholic countries during times of upheaval and great political fights, an obvious sign of the decline of societies. At the bottom of it is nothing more than legal concubinage, a shameful concession to lust, a lack of the most sacred religious and moral duties.

Finally, marriage, as a civil contract, can be undone, but as a sacrament, it is indissoluble. This is affirmed by the Savior Himself and the holy fathers. Although these men have not given the *compliments* so opportunely cited by Señorita Castro, I do not see a reason to advocate civil marriage, which puts civilization in danger and degrades society, bringing it to primitive times in which the woman was considered an object of pleasure and was scorned by everyone in old age.

I respect and admire the woman who, unable to live with her husband, separates from him, dedicating herself solely to educating her children, and *waiting* resigned, but without desiring *the death of her husband*, and once the chain has been broken, she does not ever think about making herself a prisoner again. Señorita Castro should know that once one has true love, one can never forget it.

MARÍA DOLORES TORRES
Widow of García Vivanco
Ciudad Rodrigo, 20 January 1904

Señora Colombine:

Dear señora: the limited space of one article only allows me to state for the record, in an almost telegraphic way, my defense of the perpetuity of marriage, justifying the two celebrated phrases of Bonal. Occupying himself with this matter, he says, "The Turks, with polygamy, *purchase* their neighbor's daughter; we, with divorce, *rob* our friend of his companion."

Only an incorrect idea of what marriage is and what it means can serve as a basis for divorce.

Marriage IS NOT A CONTRACT. The law of marriage is the law of love; this is a woman's life and, we might say, even her religion, since she was born to love and sacrifice herself for her beloved.

The anxiety, uncertainty, jealousy, and fears of the lovers become true, peaceful love of the husband and wife when their hopes, dreams, and yearnings become reality. Nothing is purer and more holy than this mysterious turmoil born in the heart of an honorable woman, which peeks out through her eyes, veiled by modesty, and which

146

constitutes this celestial delight that makes affection into something spiritual.

Precious jewel, absolutely delicate adornment, which should always be the woman's most precious attire—this constitutes her most delicate adornment.

The Germanic people, according to Tacitus, believed there was something divine in a woman's love, and our caballeros from the Middle Ages, in the heat of battle, dedicated themselves to their ladies.

We must distinguish between love and passion, the latter being defined by the Roman philosopher as an "emotion of the spirit opposed to reason and contrary to Nature."[114] Love purifies passion, a mysterious fire that turns the family into a true sanctuary in which the united hearts of the husband and wife are the altar, and as a real manifestation of this indissoluble union, from the fusion of two beings into one, the children appear, those earthly angels that bring happiness and delight to the life of the married couple, bringing to it a blessing from heaven.

Today let us set only this premise to resolve the trial of divorce: "Marriage *is not a contract*; the law that rules it is love."

FERNANDO COLOM

---

114. Cicero, book 4 of the *Tusculan Disputations*.

Señora Colombine:

Dear señora: I must admit that the discussion that has begun to emerge in the pages of *Diario Universal* on divorce greatly interests me. Let me say this better: it doesn't just interest me, it excites me, because I see in this a magnificent occasion for the nobility of our Spanish ladies to shine, religious ladies by tradition and by principle, who must put themselves on the side of justice, and justice is not in favor of divorce.

But I believe this discussion should pull at the roots or the foundations of the issue, roots or foundations that are certainly not arguments regarding the *advantages and disadvantages* of divorce but rather the *justice or injustice* of it.

It is not possible, with this matter of vital importance, in which not only the fortunes of the family but also the rights of the children and the honor of the upright conscience are in play, to limit ourselves to the *utilitarian* school that has been so victorious in the arena of philosophy and reason.

How many things may be *advantageous* to me, which I cannot, justly, acquire! The treasury of another may be very *advantageous* to me, but *justice* forbids me to rob. Also, divorce may be *advantageous* to many married couples, especially those that are based on the fire of overexcited passions or in the arguments between spouses necessarily caused by bonds that obeyed, not the law of true love, but the iron tyranny of the most repugnant avarice; but, although divorce may be *advantageous* in these cases, *justice* is opposed to breaking bonds that, by all accounts, are holy.

I believe, therefore, that the crux of the matter is this: marriage, before being a sacrament and a religious contract, and much before being a civil contract, is a natural contract, and precisely because of this primeval character, marriage is *indissoluble*. When all pure loves tend to perpetuate themselves, it cannot be demonstrated that conjugal love, which occupies a place of honor among these loves, is suitable for termination.

For me the question boils down to this dilemma: Either marriage is based on true, rational love and the mutual understanding of the moral qualities of the contracting parties or it is not based on this prior understanding, but rather on the basis of desire and profit, which are as excellent for commercial partnerships as they are wrong when it comes to marriage partnerships.

First, marriage tends to perpetuate itself because all pure loves perpetuate themselves. Second, it does not follow to fight the indissolubility of marriage. Rather, if the spouses realize that they originally distorted the purposes of the contract, then they (never the children) are called upon to bear the *penance* that arises from their *sin*.

EDUARDO MARTÍNEZ BALSALOBRE
Priest

Of all the opinions I have read in *Diario Universal*, the one that I loved the most was Father Martínez Balsalobre's, because its form is well expressed and because Balsalobre presents the matter on the basis of one of several points that can be used to sustain his point.

I know that arguments will not be tolerated here, but Father Balsalobre, or any other señor, could put our doubts to rest, so we might more clearly understand this *trial*.

If before being a sacrament, a religious contract, and a civil contract, marriage is *a natural contract*, let us not take nature out of things, and let us not want to make things indissoluble that by their nature cannot be, since in nature, everything is altered, everything changes, and everything evolves. And tyranny, in my humble opinion, consists of tying two beings together forever when they have joined together out of pure love (not too much, though!), and this love changes because things in nature evolve, or when two beings have joined together out of avarice or a simple mistake.

And in reality, is it *fair and just* for two people to bear penitence if, obeying the will of others, they married without love? Or if they married when they were eighteen- or twenty-year-old kids who didn't know what they were doing? No. *Justice* cannot oppose divorce in such cases. It would oppose a marriage based on *convenience*, which must not have been entirely sacred, and this is where the doubts arise, which I mentioned earlier.

If we go deeper, if we really *dig deeper* into the matter, we will see that Catholicism has been and still is the biggest enemy of marriage.

Don't be scared. Evidence? Here you go.

Let's listen to Saint Paul: "He who is unmarried cares for the things of the Lord—how he may please the Lord. But he who is married cares about the things of the world—how he may please his wife. The unmarried woman cares about the things of the Lord, that she may be holy both in body and in spirit. But she who is married cares about the things of the world—how she may please her husband, and her interests are divided."[115]

There cannot be a greater condemnation of marriage.

Tertullian, the celebrated doctor of the Catholic Church, says that remarriage is *adultery*. In the *Feast of the Virgins*, Saint Methodius teaches that chastity is *superior to matrimony*. The Council of Valencia (year 374) punished women who have forgotten their promise of chastity with two years of penance. From here we move on to Saint Augustine, Saint Anthony, Saint Hilary, Saint Basil, and even Saint Gregory of Nyssa, who said that we should *flee from pleasure* and that *we cannot understand perfection without continence*. We could fill volumes with the verdicts of the church fathers condemning marriage.

And I won't mention Saint Ambrose, who *holds the record* in this holy work. If we move forward a little to the

---

115. All but the last clause of this translated quotation comes from 1 Cor. 7.32–34. See *The Bible*, New King James Version, Thomas Nelson, 1975; *Bible Gateway*, www.biblegateway.com.

Middle Ages, we find Saint Gregory, the author of *Morals*, which says, "Unable to execute the conjunction without carnal delight, the husband and wife should abstain from entering into a sacred place for a time, *since the conjunction cannot be without blame.*"

I won't continue because the enumeration of references would be endless, but from all of this we may see that the Catholic religion is the enemy of marriage, considering it a compromise akin to a necessary evil, and yet it endeavors to make *the conjunction that cannot be without blame* indissoluble.

Notice, Señora Colombine, that I am not talking about *utilitarianism*, which we cannot do without in life.

If marriage is a *sin*, and we cannot go to the Lord through it, many can go to him with divorce, undoing the mistake and not doing it ever again. Sincerely,

A. S.
Lawyer

Señora Colombine:

Esteemed señora: Please permit me to throw in my two cents on the issue of divorce, since as a professor of Morality I explain it to my university students every year. In Spain, the Church and State recognize an incomplete divorce: separation of bodies, children, and assets; but a frequent consequence of this is the impoverishment of some couples, and I blame the husbands more than the wives; but it is upsetting that some with the vocation of wife must live as if they were single. This evil may have a civil solution, but never a religious one, since the Church considers canonical marriage a sacrament that cannot be broken.

The State should grant freedom to couples married civilly, since this doesn't jeopardize the Church, and the fact that the most cultured and advanced nations have instituted divorce should serve as an argument for it.

Well I know that in Spain marriages that are purely civil are extremely scarce, since families and the prospective brides themselves decline to get married this way. And we have seen that suitors who decline spiritual aid will compromise at the decisive moment, confessing and accepting a canonical marriage.

Nonetheless, this is not an objection; every canonical marriage is also a civil marriage, and divorce can be supported on this basis.

Any statesman who wants to establish divorce in Spain has at his disposal the means to prove the advantages of this social institution by studying the morality that prevails in couples that tolerate each other despite their infidelities, those that separate amicably or legally, and those that regain their liberty through divorce.

The trial of divorce must be founded on convincing evidence, and separation must not be based on mere whims; therefore, divorce is not an attack on the family rooted in the passions of the husband and wife.

Señora Colombine, please excuse the bother, respectfully yours,

ANTONIO JIMENO CARIDAD

Yesterday and Today
Shall We Divorce?

Colombine has unearthed an old question in *Diario Universal* that always ends up being new in Spain. Do we allow or do we not allow divorce? Is it or is it not advantageous? Should it be made law or should the door to it be
closed forever? I have here the point to be debated; I have
here the issue that, now fully in the twentieth century,
after being debated ad nauseum, has the privilege of appearing fully rejuvenated. Just as we suffer bouts of amne-
sia, everything old from bygone years must take on a
character of novelty to us. The return of the hoop skirt,
and we might exclaim, "Have you seen the things they
invent?" In the same way, a respected wife, newspaper in
hand, saw fit to remark, "This thing Colombine came up
with is a great thing." Meanwhile a sweet young woman
who was on her path to happiness complained, in a bad
mood, "Can you believe what ridiculous things they come
up with these days?" Explanations that, naturally, are in
tune with the present or future circumstances of the interested parties, or their respective unhappy or prosperous
situations. They will manifest their greater or lesser intel-

ligence and their most clever touches of pleasant argumentation, sometimes praising the indissoluble bond with Saint Paul, the Gordian knot of existence, sometimes, if they are indifferent or fickle, understanding marriage as a simple "occupation of monkeys," as Leo Tolstoy says. And thus the matter will be resolved—the matter of how to pass the time, the eternal and almost the only real issue for Spaniards, as someone once said. To revive it, there's nothing like returning to old, forgotten things. Colombine understands this well: this is her touchstone.

———

And yes, it is old! Cabarrús[116] comes to mind, that good count who, with his predecessor Macanaz and his partner Jovellanos, nourished the French encyclopedists; that good count who is not as well known as he should be, maybe because his effigy is reserved for banknotes, less accessible to most; that good count who was the first to defend divorce—and with spirit—as a man who gave much to our society. Let's listen to how he expressed his observations on the agriculture bill. It but seems that he, foreseeing the future existence of Colombine, wanted to

———

116. Francisco Conde de Cabarrús founded the Banco de San Carlos, precursor to the Bank of Spain. In the 1790s he wrote letters and reflections to Gaspar Melchor de Jovellanos, a Spanish author, philosopher, and statesman during the Enlightenment, and these letters were published in 1802. This excerpt is from "Carta quinta: Sobre la sanidad pública" ("Fifth Letter: On Public Health"); see *Cartas sobre los obstáculos que la naturaleza, la opinion y las leyes oponen a la felicidad pública*, 3rd ed., Imprenta de Burgos, 1820, pp. 277–81; *Institutional Repository*, Bank of Spain, repositorio.bde.es.

leave another reply to this plebiscite in his famous letters, as substantive as this:

"A well-furnished, happy, and pure marriage is a phenomenon of the comfortable classes, and seemingly concentrated in those hovels where the seduction of gold is inaccessible is naivete and the infections of our garrisons. In addition, adultery reigns with impunity everywhere; when not vice and prostitution, separation and divorce are the evils that accompany it. All these relaxed morals, the precise effect of the indissolubility of marriage, are not so certain when it comes to legislation; what each person observes, says, and repeats in private and public is brazenly denied when it comes time to counsel the government; in a word, the ruin of our customs does not require more attention than in useless private speeches; but divorce scares us.

"Nevertheless, I ask any sincere man to tell me if he is completely secure enough with himself to promise to always love one woman and no other; to tell me if he does not feel in his heart that the best possible means of fastening his love to one person is with the suspicion of losing that love; to tell me if, in the case that this suspicion does not stop him, public morality and he, for the sake of his welfare, are more interested in making sure he does not enslave the woman he no longer loves and that he marries the woman who promises him more happiness; and to tell me if the mother's care for her first children cannot be restored better with more happiness than with the terrible examples of a bad marriage. Finally, I beg you, summing up the advantages and disadvantages—and in this lies the perfection of humanity—decide where you find greater benefit: in divorce or in the current state of our customs?

"Divorce would restore our customs, giving a new incentive to souls that are too fortunate to recognize the problem with an indissoluble union, and it would not affect good marriages; it would impede the misfortune of many, who only stop being happy because strong passions need the continuous agitation of hope and fear; finally, it would remedy bad marriages, preventing the excesses and the lamentable consequences caused by them.

"But is it possible that our religion contradicts this demonstration of morals and logic? I open the code, and in the mouth of its divine Author I find, unequivocally, a text that refutes the theologians. Jesus Christ expressly permits divorce in cases of adultery. History shows that divorce was tolerated and authorized in the first centuries of the Church. The argument that marriage is a sacrament is as weak as the others—nothing stops this sacrament from being repeated, as is the case with remarriage, whether because of death or impotence or other causes considered just.

"Finally, in favor of divorce is morality, the interest of humanity, the authority of the Founder of our religion, history, reason, while I see against it only absurd and contradictory commentators and stupid customs; however, Your Honor knows that four years before France destroyed this terrible mistake, I had dared denounce it here in my newspaper: such is the repugnance it has always caused me."

This was how the count spoke in the last days of Charles III.

—

Ghost of Cabarrús, I salute you! Look, from where you stand (may it be in holy glory), at how ahead of your time you were, how multiple quills are still debating divorce, which is as inaccessible to Spanish legislation now as it was then, although today the debate is between idlers rather than statesmen. And don't be upset, for if this pleb-iscite has shown anything, it is that hypocrisy and decep-tion still walk triumphant on the earth. If there are con-jugal dramas, they happen as hidden as possible behind private curtains, so that ignorance precludes scandal. And you know that on top of this, they do not yearn for divorce in one hundred gilded mansions, where the apathetic lady of the house will say as she shows you around, "My rooms. My husband's. From here to there, two kilometers of hallways."

Is this not, in fact, a moral divorce?

FRANCISCO AZNAR NAVARRO

Señora Colombine:

Dear señora: I know how to feel, not how to express. I doubt, as is natural, that you will publish my opinion, which is braver than the one of the señora de P., because one needs bravery to face the label of hypocrite, which of course some advocates of divorce have baptized us, advocates that because they are miserable believe they will be happier if they stop being Christians. They are wrong: misery follows all who are born wherever they go.

The Catholic woman has no other love and no other law than the one that permits her beliefs. If one makes a mistake in her choice of companion, the children, if there are any, can be a consolation, and if not, then the satisfaction of doing one's duty can serve that purpose, and let the masses judge it as they wish. A woman's conscience, clean of all stain, will give her the courage to calmly await death.

It is well known that divorce existed before Christ, but nevertheless, in *The Travels of Antenor in Greece and Asia*, I read the following: "Most husbands only think of having their wife's children in order to perpetuate their name: they join with them only so that they will take care of the housekeeping, and reserve their attentions and courteous desires for the mistresses they keep."

Doesn't something like this happen today? We can do very much for future generations. Let us teach our children to be altruistic. Where there are no egoists, there will be no hypocrites or materialists, who, while manifesting themselves differently, are the same person.

Yours truly,

VENTURA QUINTANA

Señora Colombine:

I declare frankly that I love the idea of divorce. In Spain, where men are evil, like everywhere, and women have less liberty than in any other civilized nation, if marriage could be undone, we women would doubtless be happier—faced with the fear of losing us, men would understand that the value of an honorable and affectionate woman merits the sacrifice of his disdain and betrayals.

Also, women, especially in the middle class, are the slaves of a poorly understood duty, and the purest and most sincere friendship is often condemned by the same society that pardons the man his most intolerable slips.

I believe divorce would fall like lovely dewdrops in many homes, where sometimes the woman lives in continuous suffering.

ROSA TORRE

Señora Colombine:

Dear esteemed señora: When you initiated the trial of divorce, I of course supposed I was in favor of it, but I thought this would be about impartially gauging various opinions given voluntarily and then consulting men who would represent the political-religious-social ideas of Spain, starting with Pablo Iglesias, then moving on to Salmerón, Canalejas, Montero Ríos, Moret, Romero

Robledo, Silvela, Maura, Pidal, Nocedal, and Mella. This must not have been the case since their opinions have not appeared, and since none of them would be discourteous to a señora, I assume they haven't been consulted. In contrast, I have seen the opinions of Estévanez, Dicenta, and so on, which were requested by you, and of course favorable for divorce. The reason for this could be the desire to bring together many opinions in support of the idea in order to begin, on this basis, a campaign in favor of divorce. An enterprise that in my view is unnecessary, since today in our misfortunate Spain, civil marriage is established, and this can be dissolved easily, or if there are still difficulties with this, we could accept Masonic marriage, which you have described so well and illustrated with doodles in the *Diario*.

But that is not what this is about. Canonical marriage that can be broken is wanted, yes, for the sake of social conventions; something like a fig leaf to cover the nudity of the spirit and the flesh. A futile task; the discontented are few, but even if they were many, it would be like beating a dead horse, because the divine institutions are not moved, nor do they change their laws or procedures because of a journalistic campaign, whether it be muted, open, or violent.

Respectfully yours,

ANGEL MARÍA ACEVEDO

Señora Colombine:

I consider the legal separation of spouses by dissolution of the bond *quod ad vinculum*[117] to be a highly important question because, since the family is the cornerstone of society, it would cause new problems in the ethical-legal sphere, as occurred in Rome at the end of the republic and the beginning of the empire, where divorce became so frequent it was excessive, and it became necessary, in order to contain the chaos, to establish new laws that were as harsh as the Lex Caducaria,[118] which prohibited an emancipated woman who was married to her patron to divorce against the will of her husband.

Respectfully,

ÁNGEL LÓPEZ APARICIO

I am in favor of divorce; what is more, if the man is free, why shouldn't the woman be? And if the two are free, why shouldn't love be free?

Some would say that free love does not create a home, but in this case, why worry about the children? If you give them to Maura to raise and take care of, it's fixed.

---

117. *Divortium quo ad vinculum* is the Catholic Church's characterization of divorce; see also note 52.

118. Established in ancient Rome in 9 CE, these laws were intended to strengthen the institution of marriage.

If you believe this frank opinion is worthy, feel free to publish it. I thank you in advance. Respectfully yours,

BONIFACIO DE ANDRÉS

The civil laws of almost all nations on earth, considering marriage a simple contract between two people, have consigned to their code the right to divorce for various reasons and with all its consequences, and today the most civilized, Christian nations, including some Catholic nations, enjoy this right.

H. ALCAIDE

The first days of marriage are happy, but because the bond was contracted by force, the couple that should enjoy complete happiness, since that is why they joined together and swore eternal love, find that their happiness is exchanged within a certain space of time for coldness, abandon, insults, and finally hate. When this happens, they need compensation, a remedy, and this in my judgment is "The Divorce," which would prevent innumerable couples, who had loved each other in bygone days—the best days, according to the poet—from playing such an evil role in society.

Very truly yours,

TOMÁS VILLAR Y GUERRA

Señora Colombine:

Dear señora: I understand that divorce as a custom would be willingly accepted by the majority.

I believe in some cases it is hypocrisy to invoke our religion as the principal weapon against it, since our religion also forbids married men from being unfaithful, despite which we constantly learn of many who, not finding in their homes the happiness they had dreamed of, look outside it for consolation, to the grave detriment, on occasion, of the future of their families.

Wouldn't it be more moral if they could break the chains they found too heavy, legally creating gentler bonds in their place?

Those who because of divorce find themselves free, and whose religious convictions prevent them from remarrying, could remain free, just like many widows and widowers who for various reasons do not wish to marry again.

FE ALÍS

Señora Colombine:

Should the law admit divorce or not? That is the question, as it has been presented today. And I believe that first we should study the motives, the reason why many desire the legal sanction of divorce. The cause is the large number of unhappily married couples that exist at the present time. Why do they exist? Here we have the key, here we have the quiddity of the problem.

Let's listen to Max Nordau on marriage: "It has become a mutual agreement in which there is no more room for love than in the partnership contract of two capitalists entering upon some new business enterprise together. The pretext for marriage is still as ever, the preservation of the species, its theoretical presupposition is still the mutual attraction of two individuals of opposite sexes, but in reality, a marriage is contracted not in the interests of the future generation but solely with regard to the personal interests of the contracting parties. The consecration of morality and anthropological justification are utterly lacking in the modern marriage, especially among the so-called better classes. Marriage ought to be the victory of altruism, but it is the victory of egoism."[119]

That is to say, the only thing that can logically lead to modern marriage has disappeared from it: love; the instinct for preservation of the species, transmitted from generation to generation; great affection, which is the only thing that excuses faults, and pardons, and suffers, and makes men and women resigned.

---

119. Max Nordau was an early Zionist. Quotations of his work are from *The Conventional Lies of Our Civilization*, Laird and Lee, 1886, p. 274; the translator is anonymous.

Further on, Nordau says that today, people "get married to have their combined fortunes make life more agreeable, to provide themselves with a pleasanter home, to secure and maintain social prestige, to satisfy their vanity and to enter upon the privileges and enjoyments which society refuses to the single woman and concedes to the married one."

And is none of this love? What is the origin of this degradation of our feelings? Society itself with its absurd conventions and terrible needs, increasing every day.

Triumphant egoism: the denial of all help to those in need and fallen. What does this society do to give aid to helpless women? Imagine a poor woman who does not get married. How does she live? Where does she earn her daily bread? By occupation, work. But can every woman live by working when there are so few available jobs? Where are all these extensive workshops and jobs? No, the woman is miserable from the moment she is born in this society. Liberty does not exist for her; her life is one of slavery; and if she does not come to get married, at least a regular marriage, she will probably fall into vice and the brothel. She will be just another victim of the egoism of men.

Therefore, egoism must disappear; love must dominate in the relations between the sexes. As Schopenhauer says, "A man who marries for money, and not for love, lives more in the interest of the individual than in that of the species; a condition exactly opposed to truth; therefore it is unnatural and rouses a certain feeling of contempt. A girl who against the wish of her parents refuses to marry a rich man, still young, and ignores all considerations of *convenience*, in order to choose another instinctively to her liking, sacrifices her individual welfare to the species. But it is for this very reason that she meets with a certain approval, for she has given preference to what was more important and acted in the spirit of nature (of the species), more exactly; while the parents advised only in the spirit of individual egoism."[120]

And so, if we act according to noble thoughts and natural instincts, distanced from clumsy desires and pernicious motives, then the time will have come to find out if the institution of marriage is as bad as some people paint it. Today, yes it is; today the yoke is very harsh, and the duties great, and the disappointments many. But that is because society itself is to blame for its own wretchedness.

Leave hearts free; don't imprison them for petty, groundless reasons. It is better, much better, to create robust, healthy citizens than weak, decadent beings, even if they have titles of nobility. The races will not be saved with escutcheons but by their own hand. The land is not farmed except by spilling our sweat to make it fertile.

E. LA-GASCA

120. This quotation comes from Arthur Schopenhauer's "Metaphysics of Love"; see *Essays of Schopenhauer*, translated by Rudolf Dircks, Walter Scott, 1890; *Project Gutenberg*, 2020, www.gutenberg.org.

Señora Colombine:

Dear señora: First of all, I should say that I am the irreconcilable enemy of marriage, and therefore of divorce. Divorce means the recuperation of the freedom lost in marriage, but since actually and truly, when we join together in matrimony, this freedom is not lost, despite the codes and canonical stipulations, this is why I am against divorce, which would mean the legalization of marriage.

Excuse any bother this may have caused you. Your admirer,

LORENTE DE SANRUPERTO

Señora Colombine:

I am in favor of divorce, that is, the individual liberty of each of the contracting parties to correct the mistake they made and live as we all have the right to live: in peace and tranquility.

SALUSTIANO GÓMEZ

Señora Colombine:

Divorce will be judged the way marriage is understood.

C. VELASCO

Señora Colombine:

It is clear that divorce is not for happily married couples who enjoy the peace and pleasures of the family. Divorce is for unhappily married couples, for spouses that can't stand each other, who live in a state of constant hostility.

For these couples, I believe divorce is not only true justice but also an imperative necessity to avoid a greater evil; we should not believe anybody to be so evil as to deny a suffering creature a means to save themselves, just as a sick patient is given medicine for a cure. Divorce is a remedy for an extreme evil.

ALBERTO CASTRO GIRONA

Señora Colombine:

If marriage is by virtue of a natural law, divorce is by virtue of another natural law, and if humanity declines to impose the laws of nature, nature will survive, imposing its laws regardless. The divorce law is not a novelty. The Mosaic Law on repudiation may be a clumsy law, but it is a divorce law. So it would be advantageous to place limits on this practice and channel it so that its consequences are as painless as possible, which are nonetheless always painful. But there will always be an element of *the lesser of two evils*.

ALEJANDRA BARBERA E ISLA

Just because there is divorce in various foreign nations, that is not a reason it should be established in Spain—we must rid ourselves of the custom that *a foreign stamp legitimizes the brand*.

The Spanish woman continues to be, and rightly so, *a heroine of love*, and at the same time I advise mothers that to avoid marital discord, they should inculcate their daughters in a special way, so that they, unlike what is common today, introduce themselves to their suitors exactly as they are, so that nobody can say one woman is suited to be a girlfriend and another a wife.

ANTONIO VÁZQUEZ DE LA TORRE

It should be absolutely prohibited for our sex to marry before the age of twenty-three; a woman who has been raised to be timid is practically a girl without any experience before this age. When she marries at seventeen or eighteen, she tends to feel the consequences later and becomes miserable.

I repeat, I enthusiastically associate myself with the idea of divorce.

Sincerely,

ANDREA GÓMEZ

Considering our current customs, divorce imposes itself, but we gain nothing. When a man justly repudiates his wife, society applauds; when a wife, tired of suffering in silence the betrayals with which her husband insults and sometimes even slanders her, when she is mistreated in word and in deed, and she complains, society condemns her. How many unhappy women die of pain in some corner only because we blame the victim!

While courtesans are praised, the honorable woman is miserable with or without divorce, as long as she, lacking experience, chooses for her life's companion a man who does not know how to understand or appreciate her.

LEONOR FERRER
Reus, 11 February 1904

Señora Colombine:

France has spent the last twenty years experimenting. Maybe twenty years is not long enough to perceive the advantages of normalizing the moral status of the family, but though not the advantages, France has been demonstrating the disadvantages quite clearly for some time.

MIGUEL SÁNCHEZ
Salamanca, February 1904

If this is only about satisfying those who, being unhappy in their marriage, find on their path—he another woman, she another man—then let's give them legalized happiness through the institution of divorce; nothing is more beautiful or more moral.

ANA MATESANZ
Zaragoza

Señora Colombine:

Without doubting that one of those ideas, the most grandiose, resides in you, which is progress in consonance with civilization, with the countries at the vanguard of the enlightened world, I will allow myself to express my humble opinion on how useful and beneficial it would be to establish a divorce law in Spain, like in France and many other countries.

I consider this a law of *equality* and the most just of any that have been established since the beginning of the world because it is redemptive of the evils that corrode our society today.

GUMERSINDO ROMERO

Señora Colombine:

Let's stop the unfounded and ridiculous everyday preoccupations, and, making way for reason and common sense, let's ask for the divorce law to be established soon. It is as necessary as other laws currently in effect in Spain are useless.

Sincerely,

EUSTAQUIO MARTÍN

Señora Colombine:

I don't think divorce will ever be established in Spain. At least I don't think we will ever live to see it: the deeply religious woman will never ask for it, and men who basically don't care about these imperfections are too comfortable to ask for something new.

CARMEN DOMÍNGUEZ

Señora Colombine:

I am in favor of divorce, although not as it has been established in North America or France, but how it is, or was, in Russia, that is, only an innocent may have the right to remarry. The guilty one will have this punishment, and this way there will be no mistake made when the innocent marries another man or woman.

MARIUCHA

Divorce does not and cannot exist when the bond is what must exist.

DE SANTA BARBARA

Many have seen in the children an impediment to the establishment of divorce, saying that in cases when it is put into practice, the situation of the descendants becomes extremely anomalous, and also that their moral upbringing will suffer greatly with the pernicious example of the parents. Both things are true and undisputable, but by chance, is the situation of the children less abnormal in a case where perhaps there is an *amicable* separation of the spouses, which is very frequent today, and also an *amicable* union of one former spouse with someone else? Is by chance, the example of *unhappily married* couples less pernicious, with the constant quarreling and living in perpetual scandal?

No. Neither this, nor any other reasons justify not immediately establishing divorce, which in today's day is a true necessity. Now, it is to be expected that humanity should make notable advancements in its path of progress, that a day will come when divorce will be unnecessary because all men will know how to exercise their rights and fulfill their duties, without offense or harm to others, and that will be the day that the biblical text becomes evident, *erunt dus in carne una*,[121] because indeed, the husband and wife will know how to act in such a way as to constitute a single being with the same aspirations, with identical desires, with equal ideas and feelings.

ENRIQUE DE CÁRDENAS Y MOYA
Lawyer

The woman, when she divorces, on top of looking ridiculous, loses much honor. It is rare to find someone who will blame the separation on the man, basing their assumption—and they are not wrong—on the fact that the woman has, or should have, the duty to resign herself, suffer the idiosyncrasies of her husband, and attract him, with means that a virtuous woman always has in excess, to a path of honor and fulfillment of the commitments they swore to at the foot of the altar.

A. DE MIRABAL

Señora Colombine:

The same thing happens with marriage laws as with other laws. Is there a lawbreaker that doesn't gripe

---

121. "The two shall become one flesh"; Mark 10.8. See *The Bible*, New American Standard Bible, Lockman, 2020; *Bible Gateway*, www.biblegateway.com.

about the penal code? Well the same thing happens with unhappy couples. Is there one that doesn't seethe about the indissoluble bond of marriage? This is only natural for one and the other. And is it for this reason, Señora Colombine, that we should all agree that these laws are harmful to society? In no way should we do so, basing our decision not only on the healthiest of social principles and civil rights for the good governance of civilized nations but also on the driving precepts of the Ten Commandments, without which neither society nor the family is possible, a most sacred bond that Jesus Christ himself instituted on earth, from which we derive all our humanitarian feelings and feelings of unity.

P. LUGO

Señora Colombine:

Divorce is contrary to the psychological laws. The soul, as an essence, rejects, even in the minds of those who desire it, this absurd antisacrament.

As the soul is dependent on reason, it is opposed to this form of advance. Is divorce moral? I believe not, at least if one considers morals as the force behind our good customs and legal actions. Therefore, *Ethics* condemns divorce.

GONZALO ARNAZ

Summary

An examination of this plebiscite shows a considerable majority in favor of divorce. In addition to what was published, 1,462 votes came from readers advocating divorce, and only 320 were against it.

We also see that men of advanced ideas expressed their opinions in favor of divorce with more enthusiasm, while those known for being fervent Catholics abstained from giving their opinions.

For the defenders of indissoluble marriage, the arguments were scant and tepid, based on *blind faith that one does not argue with.**

Divorce can be considered from three different perspectives: religious, moral, and political. From the first perspective, the conception of marriage varies according to one's creed. Discarding the fable of paradise, which Alexandre Dumas went back to when he wrote *The Question of Divorce*, and returning to more modern times, we see that in early Christianity, the opinions

* With the exception of Father Balsalobre, who, to be fair, we should admit was seeking discussion.

of the holy fathers were quite varied—while Saint Epiph-anius and Saint Ambrose allowed it, Saint Augustine re-jected it.

When the Eastern and Western Churches split, the Greek Church declared itself in favor of divorce, and to this day its dogmas recognize and allow it.

The Roman Church denies divorce, but a few of its canons, without approving of it, compromise up to a certain point in practice.

The third canon of the Council of Elvira, which took place in the fourth century, condemns the married woman not when she marries a second time but if *without prior cause* she leaves her first husband and takes another. The ninth canon does not excommunicate the woman who leaves her adulterous husband and remarries, unless *the first husband is still alive.* Meanwhile, it imposes no penalty on a husband who remarries after divorcing his wife.

In every era, divorce was allowed for the powerful, with ever-increasing causes for annulment that leave the dogma intact. In effect, annulment presupposes a fault before consummation of the union, and thus the union is considered to not have been carried out. Meanwhile, divorce is the rupture of marriage.

Every religious dogma allows separation, which differs from divorce in that it prevents a second marriage, considering that the spiritual effects of the union persist.

The Reformation adopted divorce, which today is enshrined in law in every Protestant country.

In contrast, Catholics cannot even debate an issue of dogma or faith. So the Catholic Church may allow and does allow separation and annulment but not divorce.

The issue is reduced to a matter of conscience: if the laws allow divorce, believers will never avail themselves of this law, and there will be occasion for them to be doubly rewarded, since they submitted voluntarily.

From the perspective of morals, divorce has great advantages. Some have mentioned love as an argument against divorce.

Spouses that love each other never separate, regardless of the law; this is without doubt. Is it possible to hate someone after loving them? This is a question touched on by both psychology and physiology, and experience demonstrates that this occurs all too frequently. When this is the case, natural law settles it; bodies should not be united if their spirits repel each other.

Once the husband and wife are morally divorced, it is not a long way off to betrayal, hate, unfaithfulness, and even violence. A home where two people abhor each other and know that only death can separate them is horrible.

In these conditions, it is absurd to condemn adultery. If they have the ability to separate and form a new home, and the spouses are unfaithful, the penalty should be extremely severe. But as long as the laws force them to live together, betrayal is a logical consequence; not all human beings have enough willpower to be heroes or martyrs.

From a political point of view, there are serious objections.

They say, "If couples are offered the chance to dissolve their marriage and remarry, this will cause true chaos in families, and they will be exposed to tyranny and whims."

"The fate of the children is horrible," others add. For these cases there are laws that permit divorce but that protect the innocent spouse, regulate marriage, and prevent abuse.

Abuse has always existed, with or without divorce. Repudiation existed among primitive peoples and among the Jews, Greeks, and Romans. The man, the lord, the powerful one, threw away or enslaved his wife.

Throughout history, the powerful tyrannized the weak when they stopped loving them, and it is moral to permit separation when it would put an end to this suffering.

Repudiation decreased when each repudiated woman became a burden to the State, and I say *woman* because only men had the right to repudiate.

The laws should also protect the fate of the children, and their upbringing will suffer less in a calm home, with an innocent mother and father, than among the constant battles of hate and insults.

On the other hand, separation is allowed today, and the effects are the same for the children as with divorce.

The only difference is that with separation, there is usually adultery, but in a relationship that society considers legitimate, warmth and happiness can reenter the home.

Countries where the Orthodox religion is practiced have allowed divorce for a long time. Russia, Romania,

Serbia, and Bulgaria have written it into their laws, imposing very rigorous conditions.

In England in 1859, Palmerston's government introduced a law where it was quite easily determined if the offense was caused by only one of the spouses, but if both were at fault, they were required to continue living together.

The German law eliminates the perpetual separation of bodies and allows divorce. The United States concedes divorces with a facility that approximates *free love*, and in Latin America divorce exists in almost all the republics to a greater or lesser extent.

Divorce has been legal in every canton in Switzerland since 1875; the Italian cantons of Ticino and Valais had not accepted it until then.

France established divorce in 1884, and it was finalized into law on 18 April 1886. It is granted easily by mutual agreement.

Austria is divided by ethnicity and religion, and there are Catholics and Protestants. The former are only allowed the separation of bodies, while the latter are allowed to divorce, as are Jews, though with restrictions.

Holland has a wise divorce law: it is granted five years after the separation of bodies if there has not been a reconciliation.

Only Italy, Portugal, and Spain have not established divorce, although they allow civil marriage.

The fact that we are beginning to debate the advantages of divorce among ourselves *as a new idea* shows an unfortunate backwardness.

Conclusions

Divorce is a sign of progress and is allowed in the majority of countries.

Divorce is advantageous to society and morals.

Some religions accept and some reject divorce. This depends on the individual conscience and does not concern legislators.

Our plebiscite shows that Spanish opinion is favorable to divorce, and it will doubtlessly be established here as a victory for civilization.

COLOMBINE

Notes

- Due to lack of space, we only published the most notable excerpts of some letters. We were not able to include the notable tragicomedy of Don José María Macías.
- Because it arrived too late, we were unable to publish the requested opinion of Don Miguel Cid Rey, who, after a well-reasoned study of divorce as a contract and a sacrament, stated that he was completely opposed to it.
- We have an additional 1,782 opinions, which we carefully tallied for the final result of the plebiscite. These were not published because they did not fulfill our requirements.

About the Contributors

Rebecca M. Bender is associate professor of Spanish at Kansas State University, where she teaches undergraduate and graduate courses on Spanish literature and culture. Her current book project, "Pregnant Minds and Literary Bodies: Motherhood and Feminism in Spanish Women's Narratives, 1910–39," focuses on Spanish women's engagement with motherhood and feminism in fiction. Bender's various articles on early-twentieth-century Spanish literature and visual culture examine themes such as the female body, the avant-garde's fusion of fashion and fine art, and the narrative mapping of urban spaces; she has published four articles on Carmen de Burgos. Her most recent publications center on L2 literature pedagogy and the digital humanities as well as Spanish feminism in rural communities.

Slava Faybysh was born in Ukraine and immigrated to the United States as a child. He translates from Spanish and Russian. His co-translation (with Ellen Vayner) of Ainur Karim's play *Chins Up! Shoulders Back!* won the 2022 Plays in Translation Contest, sponsored by the American Literary Translators Association. His book-length translations include the Spanish anarchist Leopoldo Bonafulla's memoir, *The July Revolution: Barcelona 1909*, published in 2021, and Elsa Drucaroff's thriller set in 1970s Argentina, *Rodolfo Walsh's Last Case*, published in 2024. His translation of Carmen de Burgos's novelette "The Russian Princess" was published in 2023 in *Virginia's Sisters*, an anthology of women's writing from the interwar period. Other short translations of his have been published in journals such as *New England Review*, the *Southern Review*, and *The Common*.